A STUDENT'S VOCABULARY OF AKKADIAN IN ASSYRIAN ROYAL INSCRIPTIONS

A Student's Vocabulary of Akkadian in Assyrian Royal Inscriptions

T. E. KELLEY AND RALEIGH HETH

EISENBRAUNS | University Park, Pennsylvania

Library of Congress Cataloging-in-Publication Data

Names: Kelley, Tyler Edward author | Heth, Raleigh C. author
Title: A student's vocabulary of Akkadian in Assyrian royal inscriptions / T. E. Kelley and Raleigh Heth.
Description: University Park, Pennsylvania : Eisenbrauns, [2025] | Includes bibliographical references and index.
Summary: "Presents frequency-based lists of Akkadian terms from Assyrian Royal Inscriptions, organized by occurrence. Designed to help students prioritize high-frequency vocabulary, the volume supports more efficient learning and improved sight-reading of texts within this specific corpus"—Provided by publisher.
Identifiers: LCCN 2025033871 | ISBN 9781646023493 hardback | ISBN 9781646023509 paperback
Subjects: LCSH: Akkadian language—Glossaries, vocabularies, etc. | Akkadian language—Word frequency
Classification: LCC PJ3525 .K45 2025
LC record available at https://lccn.loc.gov/2025033871

Printed in the United States of America
Published by The Pennsylvania State University Press,
University Park, PA 16802–1003

Eisenbrauns is an imprint of The Pennsylvania State University Press.

The Pennsylvania State University Press is a member of the Association of University Presses.

It is the policy of The Pennsylvania State University Press to use acid-free paper. Publications on uncoated stock satisfy the minimum requirements of American National Standard for Information Sciences—Permanence of Paper for Printed Library Material, ANSI Z39.48–1992.

For those who taught us Akkadian,
Joel, B, and Avi . . .

. . . and for those kings of Aššur,
whose considerable foresight enabled
the preparation of this volume.

CONTENTS

PREFACE

One of the largest and most varied textual corpora in the ancient world is that of the Akkadian language. Utilized for more than two millennia to record everything from receipts to astrological treatises to literary masterpieces, Akkadian texts stand among the most productive treasures gifted by the archaeological revolution. Nevertheless, vocabulary acquisition presents one of the most basic and fundamental challenges to learning any language, particularly for ancient languages such as Akkadian. Because vocabulary cannot be taught, but only studied by the individual student, we hope that this volume provides a means by which students can acquire a robust Akkadian vocabulary in a logical and efficient manner. And since the ability to read and understand texts is among the primary motivations for learning an ancient language, we hope that the approach presented here can help students not only acquire proficiency in Akkadian but stay passionate about the language-learning process.

This volume contains clearly organized lists of Akkadian terms, divided by how often they occur in the corpus of Assyrian royal inscriptions. Rather than memorizing lists of vocabulary designed to match the practice exercises of a given grammar or randomly acquiring words as encountered, the use of frequency as a top-level organizational tool is a time-tested way forward for students hoping to improve their vocabulary in a new language. Frequency lists enable students to focus on the most commonly encountered words so that they can acquire vocabulary more efficiently and so that their ability to sight-read texts in a given corpus is thereby improved. For example, if students learns the Akkadian terms that appear more than 600 times in the extant corpus of Assyrian royal inscriptions—just 51 vocabulary items divided in our volume into three separate, smaller lists—they will be able to recognize approximately 45% of the words they will encounter in this corpus.

More importantly, proceeding in this manner will allow students to gain sight-reading proficiency and provide a solid foundation for further reading in the larger corpus of Akkadian-language texts. The Standard Babylonian dialect used in the majority of Assyrian royal inscriptions ensures the broad transferability of the vocabulary learned in this context to other corpora. This is the dialect not only of Assyrian royal inscriptions but of major literary works such as the *Gilgamesh* epic, *Anzû*, and *Enūma eliš*. By mastering the vocabulary included in this short volume, students will gain the ability to more easily engage with the most expansive and diverse corpus of texts from the ancient world.

ACKNOWLEDGMENTS

This project was born out of a shared love for Assyrian royal inscriptions.

We began our journey with Akkadian together in the Spring of 2014 at the University of Georgia. As we progressed in our study of the Akkadian language, we grew to appreciate Assyrian royal inscriptions as one of the most unique and engaging corpora in all of Mesopotamian literature. Just as importantly, these texts—with their combination of repetition and innovation—provide an ideal corpus for sharpening the skills of beginning and intermediate Akkadian students. By ordering the vocabulary of Assyrian royal inscriptions based on word frequency, we hope that students will be able to more readily access the complexities of syntax and content that intermediate study requires.

Many similar tools exist for the study of other ancient languages (including Hebrew, Aramaic, Greek, and Latin). It is our hope that this book, in providing a comparable resource for Akkadian, proves to be a tool equally useful in the hands of the aspiring Akkadian student and the long-suffering Assyriologist.

Furthermore, the authors would like to acknowledge that this project gratefully relies on data prepared by the LMU Munich– and Humboldt Foundation–funded Official Inscriptions of the Middle East in Antiquity (OIMEA) Project. We have also benefitted from a grant provided by the Purdue University Books Initiative to support the preparation of this manuscript. Finally, the reviewers of this work provided invaluable feedback that improved the quality of this volume. We are deeply grateful to all of the above and claim sole responsibility for any mistakes that still remain in this work.

ABBREVIATIONS

AHw	*Akkadisches Handwörterbuch*. Wolfram von Soden. 3 vols. Wiesbaden: Harrassowitz Verlag, 1959–81.
aj	adjective
av	adverb
CAD	*The Assyrian Dictionary of the Oriental Institute of the University of Chicago*. 21 vols. Chicago: The Oriental Institute of the University of Chicago, 1956–2006
CDA	*A Concise Dictionary of Akkadian*. Edited by Jeremy Black, Andrew George, and Nicholas Postgate. 2nd rev. ed. Santag Arbeiten und Untersuchungen zur Keilschriftkunde 5. Wiesbaden: Harrassowitz Verlag, 1999.
cnj	conjunction
det	determinative
dp	demonstrative pronoun
ip	independent pronoun
j	interjection
mod	modal particles
n	noun
nu	number
ORACC	Open Richly Annotated Cuneiform Corpus
prp	preposition
qp	interrogative pronoun
rel	relative pronoun
RIAo	Royal Inscriptions of Assyria online. https://oracc.museum.upenn.edu/riao/index.html
RINAP	Royal Inscriptions of the Neo-Assyrian Period. https://oracc.museum.upenn.edu/rinap/
rp	reciprocal pronoun

sbj	subordinate pronoun
unk	unknown
v	verb
xp	indefinite pronoun
(i), (ii), etc.	particular meaning of homophonous lexemes (see *CDA*)

HOW TO USE THIS BOOK

The corpus of Assyrian royal inscriptions spans over 1,500 years, from the late third millennium to the mid-first millennium. These texts record the deeds of the kings of Assyria—their titulary, their military campaigns, and their building projects. The corpus of these inscriptions contains approximately 214,000 words—excluding proper nouns such as the names of gods or cities—representing over 4,000 separate lexemes (for information on how this data was acquired, see the next section; for a broader view of the data contained in this volume, see appendix H).

This book is divided into ten chapters, with each chapter subdivided into distinct lists. In the interest of facilitating vocabulary learning, we have endeavored to keep these lists relatively short (i.e., approximately thirty entries or fewer per list). This will allow students to focus on studying a manageable number of words at a time while not becoming overwhelmed.

Within each list, the lexemes are arranged by decreasing frequency rather than alphabetically or by part of speech. As students progress through the chapters of this book, they should try to master the terms in each list to the best of their ability. In doing so, they will increase their ability to sight-read Assyrian royal inscriptions without needing to consult additional resources such as dictionaries or lexica as frequently.

Every entry in chapters 1–9 includes four pieces of information: (1) the Akkadian lexeme, (2) the lexeme's part of speech (given as abbreviations corresponding to their ORACC classification), (3) a sample of English translations for the Akkadian lexeme, and (4) the number of times each lexeme occurs in the corpus of Assyrian royal inscriptions. Note also that those Akkadian words that can be written logographically will be rendered in **bold**; students should consult appendix E for the corresponding logographic writings.

Here is an example entry using the noun ilu ("god"):

ilu (n.) god | 2,156

In addition to the above, verbs will also include their respective vowel classes listed alongside their part of speech. For a detailed description of vowel class markings and their meanings, see the introduction to appendix C. Here is an example entry using the verb alāku ("go; march; walk"):

alāku (v.; a-i) go; march; walk | 1,256

At the bottom of each list, users will also find a section for taking their own notes. We recommend that students use this section to practice vocabulary terms, record additional meanings of words, or copy out memorable sentences they have encountered containing the word(s) in the list.

Chapter 10, which contains words occurring fourteen to five times, is organized differently from chapters 1–9. Here users will find a running list of terms subdivided by number of occurrences. This format is due to the large number of words that occur at these specific frequency rates. It is recommended that students focus less on memorizing all elements of these entries and more on gaining a general acquaintance with them. In other words, while students should endeavor to memorize the lists contained in chapters 1–9, a different approach should be taken to the vocabulary in chapter 10. As these words constitute only 3.79% of the words that one encounters in Assyrian royal inscriptions, students will be better served by engaging directly with the text of royal inscriptions rather than focusing on the comprehensive memorization of the lists in chapter 10. Nevertheless, perusing the lists in chapter 10 will better equip students for this encounter and can serve as an aspirational memorization set for ambitious students—particularly those interested in working with other Standard Babylonian textual corpora.

Due to the high volume of terms occurring four or fewer times, issues of space preclude us from providing entries for these lexemes. Students should consult a lexicon as they encounter such infrequently occurring terms.

Finally, this book includes a handful of appendixes that students may find useful. Appendix A contains a chart of the pronominal suffixes encountered in Standard Babylonian. While not lexeme items, these particles do represent meaningful semantic content and students should become familiar with them. Appendix B contains a brief overview of the major phonological features of the Standard Babylonian dialect of Akkadian. Although by no means comprehensive, this overview will provide introductory students with the information necessary to navigate the Assyrian royal inscriptions composed in Standard

Babylonian. Appendix C contains an alphabetical list of verbs, alongside their characteristic vowel classes. Appendixes D and E each contain an index of the logograms used in Assyrian royal inscriptions alongside their Akkadian reading, the first organized by logographic writing and the second organized by their Akkadian readings. Appendix F contains a list of all divine names and related logograms encountered in Assyrian royal inscriptions, as these figures play an important role within the corpus, and the writings of their names are frequently logographic. Appendix G contains a list of Assyrian kings, including the lengths of each individual's reign (where known) and how many extant inscriptions originate from each king's reign. Finally, appendix H contains a table of statistics further breaking down word occurrences in this corpus, which may be of interest to both students and Assyriologists more broadly.

Although working through this book on its own will undoubtedly increase your ability to read Akkadian-language texts, we highly recommend that students concurrently use texts contained in the RIAo project or in the various RINAP (or forthcoming Royal Inscriptions of Assyria) volumes to read through actual Assyrian royal inscriptions. Doing so while also using this book will allow students to increase their fluency as they work through these texts and lists in conjunction. This experience should help students remain motivated in their Akkadian language-learning journey.

METHODS AND EDITORIAL POLICIES

The raw data utilized for this work was derived from the Royal Inscriptions of Assyria online (RIAo) project contained in the Open Richly Annotated Cuneiform Corpus (ORACC). This project, then, gratefully relies on data prepared by the LMU Munich– and Humboldt Foundation–funded Official Inscriptions of the Middle East in Antiquity (OIMEA) project. The contributions by this project to the digitization of primary materials from the ancient Near East has radically advanced the study of cuneiform culture.

The editors of this book implemented the following editorial policies for the handling of this data in order to produce the lists contained here. Please note that disagreements with and changes to RIAo's own data are unmarked throughout this volume.

Headword Form

We have retained RIAo's choice of headwords that reflect the Old Babylonian spellings of words (a policy students will also encounter in, e.g., the *CDA*). Students should be aware that the majority of the texts in the corpus of Assyrian royal inscriptions are written in the Standard Babylonian form of the language and reflect various phonological changes that distinguish this form of Akkadian from the Old Babylonian most students are introduced to in grammar books. It is highly recommended that students consult appendix B before using this book, as it discusses the major features of the Standard Babylonian dialect.

Homophonous Lexemes

Homophonous lexemes were assigned an entry number corresponding with their assignment in the *CDA*. Where the RIAo data contains homophonous lexemes that do not appear in the *CDA*, they have been assigned a lexeme number that is one higher than the highest homophonous lexeme contained in the *CDA*. Occasionally, the permissible uses of a term are such that, while listed under a single entry in the *CDA*, RIAo has identified them as separate terms (e.g., kiskattû, meaning both a kiln and a craftsman, is a single lexeme in *CDA* and treated as separate lexemes in RIAo). In many of these cases we have retained RIAo's distinction and assigned lexeme numbers that correspond to the *CDA*'s subentries for the term.

Definitions of Akkadian Terms

Due to concerns for space, this book avoids providing more than four definitions per term. These encompass the broadest meanings of the word, but students should consult dictionaries when reading to assess more specific uses.

Verbs

As a general rule, this book will only provide definitions for verbs that correspond to the G-stem. For definitions of verbs as reflected in the derived stems (N, D[t/tn], Š[t/tn], etc.), please refer to the more expansive entries in the *CAD*, *CDA*, or *AHw*. Nevertheless, definitions for derived stems are provided in some specific cases where they would be especially helpful for beginning students of Akkadian.

Verbal Adjectives

As a general rule, we have retained RIAo's policy of classifying verbal adjectives as adjectives, except in cases where this creates homophonous entries (e.g., III-weak verbs).

Participles

As a general rule, we have retained RIAo's policy of classifying substantivized participles as nouns and assigned a lexeme number where necessary. Students should, however, recognize the typical participial vowel pattern (pārisu) and be able to associate it with the related verbal root.

Substantive Adjectives

While RIAo identifies substantivized adjectives as noun entries, we have chosen to subsume these under the relevant adjective entry. Students should be aware that any adjective (e.g., "fierce") can be used in a nominal way (i.e., "the fierce one").

CHAPTER I

Words Appearing More Than 600 Times

Chapter 1 at a Glance	Total Number of Words in List	Total Number of Occurrences	Percentage of Occurrences in the Corpus
List 1-A: Words occurring more than 2,000 times	13	57,805	27.01%
List 1-B: Words occurring 2,000–1,000 times	20	26,670	12.46%
List 1-C: Words occurring 999–600 times	18	13,564	6.34%
Total:	51	98,039	45.81%

Learning all the words in chapter 1 will enable you to read 45.81% of the words you encounter in Assyrian royal inscriptions.

List 1-A

Words Occurring More Than 2,000 Times

ina	(prp.) in, into; according to; against | 9,279
ana	(prp.) to, into; about, among; as | 7,432
šarru	(n.) king | 6,487
u	(cnj.) and; moreover | 5,458
ša (i)	(det.) of; concerning | 5,348
ša (ii)	(rel.) that; when; which; who; whose | 5,131
mātu	(n.) land | 4,536
ālu	(n.) city | 2,644
lā	(mod.) not | 2,499
rabû (i)	(aj.) great; large; chief; elder | 2,423
māru	(n.) son; citizen; descendant | 2,219
bēlu	(n.) lord; possessor | 2,193
ilu	(n.) god | 2,156

Notes

List 1-B

Words Occurring 2,000–1,000 Times

adi	(prp.) as far as; until; while | 1,980
ištu	(prp.) after; from | 1,903
qerbu	(n.) center; within | 1,822
epēšu	(v.; u) make; do; perform | 1,599
šakānu	(v.; a-u) put, place; establish | 1,579
šarrūtu	(n.) kingship; reign | 1,436
eli	(prp.) above; against; concerning | 1,428
kašādu	(v.; a-u) achieve; conquer; arrive | 1,305
nišū	(n.) people | 1,270
alāku	(v.; a-i) go; march; walk | 1,256
dannu	(aj.) fortified; strong | 1,193
libbu	(n.) heart; interior | 1,193
bītu	(n.) house; temple | 1,158
ēkallu	(n.) palace | 1,147
kiššatu	(n.) totality; world | 1,116
ūmu (i)	(n.) day | 1,116
šadû (i)	(n.) mountain | 1,069
šumu	(n.) name; line (of text) | 1,063
qātu	(n.) hand; portion | 1,037
itti	(prp.) with; against; at | 1,000

Notes

List ɪ-C

Words Occurring 999–600 Times

ṣabātu	(v.; a) take (over); capture; seize | 977
pānu	(n.) before; front; face; past | 931
kīma	(prp.) like, as | 899
abu	(n.) father; ancestor | 871
me'atu	(nu.) (one) hundred | 836
târu	(v.; ū) return; turn; do again | 836
ašru	(n.) place; (divine) abode; where | 807
šēpu	(n.) foot | 793
bēlūtu	(n.) lordship; rule | 784
ummānu	(n.) army; troops; labor force | 722
kakku	(n.) weapon; symbol | 703
tiāmtu	(n.) sea | 685
ḫurāṣu	(n.) gold | 649
ṣēru	(n.) against; on; open country | 641
lū (ii)	(mod.) indeed | 615
kaspu	(n.) silver; price | 607
maḫru (ii)	(n.) front; before | 607
šalālu	(v.; a-u) plunder; carry off | 601

Notes

CHAPTER 2

Words Appearing Between 599 and 220 Times

Chapter 2 at a Glance	Total Number of Words in List	Total Number of Occurrences	Percentage of Occurrences in the Corpus
List 2-A: Words occurring 599–400 times	26	12,788	5.98%
List 2-B: Words occurring 399–326 times	26	9,348	4.37%
List 2-C: Words occurring 325–276 times	24	7,303	3.41%
List 2-D: Words occurring 275–240 times	26	6,686	3.12%
List 2-E: Words occurring 239–220 times	22	5,111	2.39%
Total:	124	41,236	19.27%

Learning all the words in chapters 1–2 will enable you to read 65.08% of the words you encounter in Assyrian royal inscriptions

List 2-A

Words Occurring 599–400 Times

šallatu (n.) plunder; captive | 595
rēšu (n.) head; top; beginning | 593
wašābu (v.; a-i) reside; settle; sit | 583
maddattu (n.) tribute; payment | 579
maḫāru (v.; a-u) receive; accept; appeal to | 573
gimru (n.) all; totality | 557
iššiakku (n.) vice-regent (of a god) | 557
tāḫāzu (n.) battle array; battle | 555
šuāti (ip.) him; that | 552
līm (nu.) thousand | 512
biltu (n.) talent; tribute; load | 506
šemû (v.; e) hear; understand | 487
rubû (n.) prince; ruler | 484
šipru (n.) work; message | 483
sisû (n.) horse | 479
kânu (v.; ū) establish; impose; fix | 467
wabālu (v.; a-i) bring; carry | 461
erēbu (v.; u) enter | 448
nakru (ii) (n.) enemy | 425
ṣābū (n.) troops; people | 423
wāšibu (n.) inhabitant | 421
palû (n.) reign; regnal year; dynasty | 419
narkabtu (n.) chariot | 411
alpu (n.) ox | 407
ṣīru (i) (aj.) exalted; high-ranking | 406
kussû (n.) throne | 405

Notes

List 2-B

Words Occurring 399–326 Times

dūru (i) (n.) (city) wall | 394
manû (iv) (v.; u) count; deliver | 392
waṣû (v.; i) go out | 392
izuzzu (v.; a-i) stand; erect | 381
qabû (v.; i) say; command | 380
kalû (ii) (n.) all | 379
šaknu (ii) (n.) appointee; governor | 375
tukultu (n.) help; support; trust | 375
naqāru (v.; a-u) demolish | 371
napištu (n.) life | 367
šubtu (n.) dwelling; site; seat | 362
anāku (ip.) I | 357
nīru (n.) yoke | 357
dâku (v.; ū) defeat; kill | 356
nadû (iii) (v.; i) lay; throw (down) | 356
kanāšu (v.; u) bow down; submit | 352
napālu (v.; a-u) demolish; destroy | 348
kibru (n.) quarter; bank; region | 346
bābu (n.) gate; opening | 343
gerru (n.) campaign; road | 343
bēltu (n.) lady | 341
šūt (i) (det.) of; those of; who(m) | 340
ul (mod.) not | 340
šamû (n.) heaven | 337
redû (i) (v.; e) add; travel; lead | 335
amāru (v.; a-u) experience; inspect | 329

Notes

List 2-C

Words Occurring 325–276 Times

elû (iii) (v.; i) ascend; go up | 325
nagû (n.) district; region | 324
maḫrû (i) (aj.) former; first | 323
rapšu (aj.) wide; extensive | 323
siḫirtu (n.) entirety; surroundings | 318
ṣalmu (ii) (n.) image | 318
anāḫu (v.; a) be(come) dilapidated; be(come) tired | 317
qibītu (n.) command; speech | 317
kabtu (aj.) heavy; important | 316
zēru (ii) (n.) offspring; seed(s) | 310
ezēbu (v.; i) abandon; leave; spare | 309
malku (n.) ruler; king | 308
āliku (n.) one who goes | 304
zikru (n.) utterance; name | 304
muḫḫu (n.) skull; on; top | 302
pīḫātu (n.) governor; province | 298
erṣetu (n.) earth; underworld; territory | 296
miṣru (n.) border; territory | 296
uššu (n.) foundation | 294
ṣēnu (iii) (n.) flock; sheep (and goats) | 287
edēšu (v.; i) be(come) new; (D) renovate | 281
šūt rēši (n.) eunuch | 280
šapāru (v.; a-u) send; govern | 277
rūqu (aj.) distant | 276

Notes

List 2-D

Words Occurring 275–240 Times

bānû (n.) builder; creator | 274
lawû (ii) (v.; i) surround | 274
namāšu (v.; u) set (oneself) in motion | 274
pāṭu (n.) border | 270
qablu (i) (n.) center | 268
aḫu (i) (n.) brother | 267
siparru (n.) bronze | 265
erēnu (n.) cedar | 263
mādu (aj.) many; much; very | 263
maqātu (v.; u) fall; happen | 262
mû (n.) water | 262
liwītu (n.) environs; circumference | 261
kī (prp.) like; as; in accordance with | 260
lū (A) (mod.) may | 260
išātu (n.) fire | 258
narû (n.) stele | 256
emēdu (v.; i) stand; impose; install | 251
šiṭru (n.) writing; inscription | 249
abātu (ii) (v.; a-u) run away | 247
šuklulu (ii) (v.; Š) complete | 247
inūma (sbj.) at that time; when | 244
werû (n.) copper | 244
erbe (nu.) four | 243
būšu (n.) goods | 242
dekû (v.; e) muster; raise | 241
mušarû (n.) (royal) inscription | 241

Notes

List 2-E

Words Occurring 239–220 Times

ebēru	(v.; i) cross over | 239
mala	(prp.) as much as | 239
dabdû	(n.) defeat | 238
našû (ii)	(v.; i) carry; lift | 238
wašāru	(v.; D) abandon; release; leave | 238
nīqu	(n.) offering; sacrifice | 237
takālu	(v.; a/i) trust | 235
warkû	(aj.) later; rear guard; back | 235
ilūtu	(n.) divinity; godhead | 234
makkūru	(n.) property | 234
abnu	(n.) stone | 233
abullu	(n.) city gate | 232
balāṭu (i)	(n.) life | 232
maḫāṣu	(v.; a) fight; beat; weave | 232
šaṭāru	(v.; a-u) write; inscribe | 231
kullatu	(n.) all of | 230
qerēbu	(v.; i) approach; come close | 230
šū	(ip.) he; that | 230
damqu	(aj.) good; capable | 227
šakkanakku	(n.) (military) governor | 225
naqû	(v.; i) make an offering; pour a libation | 222
pû (i)	(n.) mouth; command | 220

Notes

CHAPTER 3

Words Appearing Between 219 and 125 Times

Chapter 3 at a Glance	Total Number of Words in List	Total Number of Occurrences	Percentage of Occurrences in the Corpus
List 3-A: Words occurring 219–200 times	22	4,596	2.15%
List 3-B: Words occurring 199–180 times	20	3,740	1.75%
List 3-C: Words occurring 179–165 times	26	4,474	2.09%
List 3-D: Words occurring 164–145 times	27	4,162	1.94%
List 3-E: Words occurring 144–125 times	24	3,171	1.48%
Total:	119	20,143	9.41%

Learning all the words in chapters 1–3 will enable you to read 74.49% of the words you encounter in Assyrian royal inscriptions.

List 3-A

Words Occurring 219–200 Times

šamšu (n.) sun | 218
epištu (n.) deed; work | 216
idu (n.) side; arm | 215
bêlu (v.; ē) rule (over) | 214
qaqqadu (n.) head | 213
anḫūtu (n.) dilapidation; tiredness | 212
išû (i) (v.; i/u) have | 212
nabû (ii) (v.; i) call; name | 212
malû (iv) (v.; a) be(come) full; (D) entrust | 211
saḫāpu (v.; a-u) overwhelm; envelop | 211
kišittu (n.) conquest; booty | 210
aššu (prp.) in order to; because; so that | 209
ešēru (v.; i) go straight ahead | 206
ḫalāqu (v.; i) escape; (D) destroy | 206
nadānu (ii) (v.; i) give | 206
nakāru (v.; i) be(come) different; be(come) hostile | 206
danānu (i) (n.) might; power | 205
napḫaru (n.) entirety; total | 205
ṣeḫru (i) (aj.) small; young | 204
nakāsu (v.; i) cut (down, off) | 203
šarāpu (v.; a-u) burn | 202
bašû (i) (v.; i) be; come into being; exist | 200

Notes

List 3-B

Words Occurring 199–180 Times

annû	(dp.) this | 198
emūqu	(n.) strength; military force | 198
šattu	(n.) year | 198
gīru	(n.) fire(-god); fire | 197
dīktu	(n.) defeat; slaughter | 193
ellu	(aj.) pure | 190
warki	(prp.) after; behind | 187
nabalkutu (ii)	(v.; N) rebel; cross over | 186
raṣāpu	(v.; i) build; erect | 186
banû (iv)	(v.; i) build; create | 184
awātu	(n.) word; matter | 183
nērebu	(n.) entrance; (mountain) pass | 183
palāḫu	(v.; a) be(come) afraid; revere | 183
šamnu	(n.) oil | 183
šīmtu	(n.) fate | 183
ikribu	(n.) prayer; blessing | 182
māḫāzu	(n.) cult center; shrine | 182
parzillu	(n.) iron | 182
šulmu	(n.) well-being; setting (of the sun); completeness | 182
līmu	(n.) eponym (of year) | 180

Notes

List 3-C

Words Occurring 179–165 Times

ēpišu	(n.) builder; doer; fashioner | 179
pīlu	(n.) limestone | 178
bēl pīḫāti	(n.) governor | 177
dannūtu	(n.) fortress; strength | 177
īnu	(n.) eye; spring | 177
mārtu	(n.) daughter | 177
nasāḫu	(v.; a-u) tear out; remove | 176
immeru	(n.) sheep | 175
leqû	(v.; e) take; accept | 175
qaštu	(n.) bow; archer; bow-star | 175
ramānu	(n.) self | 175
qaqqaru	(n.) ground; distance | 174
ṭābu	(aj.) good; sweet | 174
wâru	(v.; ā) go; (D) send; govern | 174
imēru (i)	(n.) donkey | 173
gabadibbu	(n.) parapet | 170
parakku	(n.) dais | 170
ekēmu	(v.; i) take away | 169
ḫarrānu	(n.) way; path; campaign | 168
rabû (ii)	(v.; i) be(come) great; grow up | 167
ṣītu	(n.) issue; exit; origin | 167
šaṭru	(aj.) written | 166
šiddu	(n.) side; length; area | 166
ḫuršānu	(n.) mountain(s) | 165
simtu	(n.) symbol, procedure | 165
šâšu	(ip.) him; that | 165

Notes

List 3-D

Words Occurring 164–145 Times

lītu (i)	(n.) victory; power | 164
kīnu	(aj.) reliable; true; stable | 162
ṭēmu	(n.) thought; intention; report | 162
qamû	(v.; i/u) burn (up) | 161
rašû	(v.; i) acquire; come to have | 161
qablu (ii)	(n.) battle | 160
rakāsu	(v.; a-u) bind; construct | 160
marṣu	(aj.) difficult; harsh; sick | 159
lemuttu	(n.) evil | 157
mimma	(xp.) all; any; anything | 157
birtu (i)	(n.) fort; fortifications | 156
našāqu	(v.; i) kiss | 155
tāmartu	(n.) audience gift; appearance | 155
wardu	(n.) servant; slave | 155
temmēnu	(n.) foundation; foundation document | 154
ešertu	(n.) shrine; chapel | 151
lapāni	(prp.) from before; from; on account of | 151
parû (i)	(n.) mule | 151
šinnu	(n.) tooth; ivory | 151
ammatu	(n.) a unit of length | 149
bāšû	(aj.) existing | 149
nāru (i)	(n.) river; watercourse | 149
pīru	(n.) elephant | 148
šittu	(n.) remnant | 148
qardu	(aj.) valiant; warrior-like | 147
gušūru	(n.) beam; tree-trunk | 145
petû (ii)	(v.; e) open | 145

Notes

List 3-E

Words Occurring 144–125 Times

nību (n.) number | 143
šallatiš (av.) as booty | 141
šurmēnu (n.) cypress | 140
zakāru (v.; a-u) name; speak; swear | 139
šalāmu (ii) (v.; i) be(come) well; be(come) completed | 137
šarāku (v.; a-u) present; bestow | 137
umma (prp.) saying | 137
ēkurru (n.) temple | 136
naparšudu (v.; N) flee; escape | 136
warādu (v.; a-i) go down | 134
musukkannu (n.) type of wood (Magan-tree) | 133
ištēn (nu.) one | 132
mūšabu (n.) residence | 130
tīlu (n.) (ruin) mound | 130
nibītu (n.) naming; invocation; (one) nominated | 129
labāru (v.; i) be(come) old | 127
niṣirtu (n.) treasure; secret | 127
pūtu (n.) front piece; in front of; opposite; side | 127
taskarinnu (n.) boxwood; box tree | 127
eššūtu (n.) newness | 126
ramû (ii) (v.; i) install; settle | 126
šâtunu (ip.) those | 126
zikaru (n.) male | 126
qurādu (n.) warrior | 125

Notes

CHAPTER 4

Words Appearing Between 124 and 80 Times

Chapter 4 at a Glance	Total Number of Words in List	Total Number of Occurrences	Percentage of Occurrences in the Corpus
List 4-A: Words occurring 124–112 times	26	3,060	1.43%
List 4-B: Words occurring 111–102 times	26	2,769	1.29%
List 4-C: Words occurring 101–91 times	26	2,499	1.17%
List 4-D: Words occurring 90–86 times	26	2,283	1.07%
List 4-E: Words occurring 85–80 times	28	2,306	1.08%
Total:	132	12,917	6.04%

Learning all the words in chapters 1–4 will enable you to read 80.52% of the words you encounter in Assyrian royal inscriptions.

List 4-A

Words Occurring 124–112 Times

kabattu	(n.) liver; mind | 124
lubuštu	(n.) clothing | 124
nêru (i)	(v.; ē) kill; strike | 124
qiāšu	(v.; ī) give; grant | 123
karānu	(n.) vine; wine | 122
ušû	(n.) ebony | 121
pašāšu	(v.; a-u) anoint | 120
tamḫāru	(n.) battle | 120
etēqu	(v.; i) cross (over); go past; transgress | 119
danānu (ii)	(v.; i) be(come) strong | 118
rē'û	(n.) shepherd | 118
unūtu	(n.) equipment; utensils | 118
kanšu	(aj.) submissive | 117
kiṣru	(n.) contingent; knot; bedrock | 117
aḫu (ii)	(n.) arm; shore; side | 116
itû	(n.) boundary; side | 116
šâtu	(ip.) that | 116
yâti	(ip.) me | 116
kišādu	(n.) neck; shore | 115
nawāru	(v.; i) be(come) bright; shine | 115
pāliḫu	(n.) one who fears, reveres | 115
kaṣāru	(v.; i) tie; organize | 114
mētequ	(n.) course; passage | 114
tawwertu	(n.) surrounding territory | 114
melammu	(n.) fearsome radiance | 112
migru	(n.) favorite; consent | 112

Notes

List 4-B

Words Occurring 111–102 Times

meḫretu (n.) in front of; opposite | 111
warḫu (n.) month | 111
māgiru (n.) submissive one | 110
palāsu (v.; a-u) look at | 110
rēṣūtu (n.) assistance; help | 110
adû (n.) treaty | 109
ḫadîš (av.) happily | 109
mīnu (ii) (n.) number | 109
karāšu (n.) military camp | 108
šanānu (v.; a-u) be equal | 108
naṣāru (v.; a-u) guard; keep; observe | 107
wardūtu (n.) servitude; vassalage | 107
dadmū (n.) settlements | 106
pagru (n.) corpse; body | 106
šattišamma (av.) year by year; yearly | 106
ašnugallu (n.) alabaster | 105
daltu (n.) door | 105
libittu (n.) mudbrick; brickwork | 105
pētḫallu (n.) cavalry | 105
narāmu (n.) loved one | 104
tarāṣu (v.; a-u) stretch out; roof; extend | 104
tiklu (n.) support | 104
gammalu (n.) camel | 103
kāšidu (aj.) conquering | 103
abātu (i) (v.; a-u) destroy | 102
tebû (v.; i) attack; rise up | 102

Notes

List 4-C

Words Occurring 101–91 Times

manû (i)	(n.) a unit of weight | 101
sakāpu	(v.; i) overthrow | 101
tayyartu	(n.) return | 101
watāru	(v.; i) exceed; increase | 101
warû	(v.; u) lead; bring | 100
ištaru	(n.) goddess | 99
mīlu	(n.) high water; flooding | 99
lemnu	(aj.) bad, evil | 98
aḫāmiš	(rp.) one another | 96
bēru (iii)	(n.) double hour | 96
dagālu	(v.; a-u) watch; obey; (Š) entrust | 96
eṭlu	(n.) young man | 96
tību	(n.) attack; rising | 96
birmu	(n.) multicolored cloth | 95
ebbu	(aj.) pure; bright | 95
iṣu	(n.) tree; wood | 95
nabnītu	(n.) form; creation | 95
agurru	(n.) baked brick | 94
ai (i)	(mod.) not | 94
dannatu	(n.) foundation pit; fortress | 94
iṣṣūru	(n.) bird | 94
šaknu (i)	(aj.) placed; established | 94
zaqāpu	(v.; a-u) plant; fix upright | 94
mundaḫṣu	(n.) fighter | 93
ayyābu	(n.) enemy | 91
birīt	(prp.) between | 91

Notes

List 4-D

Words Occurring 90–86 Times

annaku (n.) tin | 90
dārītu (n.) eternity | 90
mālaku (n.) course; march | 90
šaplû (aj.) lower | 90
ašarēdu (aj.) first and foremost | 89
eqlu (n.) field; terrain | 89
kullumu (v.; D) show | 89
tamšīlu (n.) replica; likeness | 89
tarṣu (n.) extent; the time of | 89
dārû (aj.) lasting; eternal | 88
sapānu (v.; a-u) flatten | 88
šangûtu (n.) priesthood; priestly duties | 88
šarāḫu (v.; D) be proud; (D) make splendid | 88
warkītu (n.) future | 88
gērû (n.) enemy | 87
ḫaṭṭu (n.) scepter | 87
kirû (n.) (fruit) plantation; orchard | 87
paḫāru (ii) (v.; u) gather | 87
šutlumu (v.; Š) grant (generously) | 87
uznu (n.) ear; wisdom | 87
ezzu (aj.) furious | 86
kitru (n.) help; ally | 86
mašku (n.) skin | 86
ṣiātu (n.) distant time | 86
tamāḫu (v.; a-u) grasp | 86
urḫu (n.) road | 86

Notes

List 4-E

Words Occurring 85–80 Times

baltūtu (n.) state of being alive | 85
retû (ii) (v.; i) install; set in place | 85
šaqû (i) (aj.) high; exalted | 85
šitkunu (aj.) situated; firmly fixed | 85
tamlīu (n.) terrace; inlay | 85
adāru (v.; a-u) be(come) afraid | 84
ṣullû (v.; D) beseech; supplicate | 84
biātu (v.; ī) spend the night | 83
eššiš (av.) anew | 83
kittu (n.) truth; justice | 83
kitû (n.) linen | 83
lamassu (n.) type of sphinx; (female) tutelary deity | 83
rēmu (n.) compassion | 83
šâlu (v.; ā) ask | 83
arāku (v.; i) be(come) long | 82
nāṣiru (n.) guard | 82
peṣû (aj.) white | 82
labāriš (av.) becoming old | 81
naʾdu (i) (aj.) attentive | 81
parṣu (n.) rite; divine office | 81
puluḫtu (n.) fear; awesomeness | 81
šīru (n.) flesh; omen | 81
šūši (nu.) sixty | 81
eleppu (n.) ship | 80
gapšu (aj.) arisen; numerous | 80
irtu (n.) breast; front | 80
lū (iii) (cnj.) either; or | 80
pašāṭu (v.; i) erase | 80

Notes

CHAPTER 5

Words Appearing Between 79 and 50 Times

Chapter 5 at a Glance	Total Number of Words in List	Total Number of Occurrences	Percentage of Occurrences in the Corpus
List 5-A: Words occurring 79–73 times	26	1,977	0.92%
List 5-B: Words occurring 72–70 times	22	1,562	0.73%
List 5-C: Words occurring 69–65 times	27	1,801	0.84%
List 5-D: Words occurring 64–60 times	26	1,619	0.76%
List 5-E: Words occurring 59–57 times	24	1,388	0.65%
List 5-F: Words occurring 56–52 times	24	1,285	0.60%
List 5-G: Words occurring 51–50 times	17	857	0.40%
Total:	166	10,489	4.90%

Learning all the words in chapters 1–5 will enable you to read 85.42% of the words you encounter in Assyrian royal inscriptions.

List 5-A

Words Occurring 79–73 Times

išdu	(n.) foundation | 79
kalāma	(n.) all (of it) | 79
nawru	(aj.) bright | 79
rīqu	(n.) aromatic substance | 79
šanû (ii)	(aj.) (an)other | 79
tabāku	(v.; a-u) pour (out); heap up | 79
elû (i)	(aj.) upper; high | 78
bēl āli	(n.) city ruler | 77
ḫīṭu (i)	(n.) crime; penalty | 77
kabāsu	(v.; a-u) tread (down); walk over | 77
sikkatu	(n.) peg; cone | 76
šiāmu	(v.; ī) decree | 76
timmu	(n.) column | 76
tupšikku	(n.) corvée labor; basket (for bricks) | 76
balāṭu (ii)	(v.; a) live | 75
dāmu	(n.) blood | 75
paqādu	(v.; i) appoint; entrust | 75
puḫru	(n.) assembly; totality | 75
šarratu	(n.) queen | 75
ušmannu	(n.) (military) camp | 75
parāsu	(v.; a-u) cut off; divide; block | 74
ṣippatu	(n.) fruit orchard | 74
rapāšu	(v.; i) be(come) wide | 73
rasābu	(v.; i) smite | 73
ṣimittu	(n.) (yoke-)team; binding | 73
šâtina	(ip.) those | 73

Notes

List 5-B

Words Occurring 72–70 Times

apsasû	(n.) zebu (humped cow); bull statue | 72
balṭu	(aj.) living | 72
mānu	(n.) counting | 72
rā'imu	(n.) one who loves | 72
saḫāru	(v.; u) go around; surround; turn | 72
sattukku	(n.) regular delivery | 72
uqnû	(n.) lapis lazuli | 72
akṣu	(aj.) dangerous; brazen | 71
batāqu	(v.; a-u) cut off; hew | 71
ebertān	(av.) on the opposite bank | 71
ewû	(v.; e) become | 71
nagbu	(n.) (the) whole; underground water | 71
namurratu	(n.) awe-inspiring radiance | 71
nisiqtu	(n.) selection | 71
ṭiābu	(v.; ī) be(come) good; be(come) pleasing | 71
biblu	(n.) desire; produce | 70
kalû (v)	(v.; a) detain; hold (back) | 70
mūšu	(n.) night | 70
nadû (i)	(aj.) situated; abandoned | 70
pitqu	(n.) refining process; cast metalwork | 70
qinnu	(n.) clan; nest | 70
sinništu	(n.) woman | 70

Notes

List 5-C

Words Occurring 69–65 Times

aḫāzu (v.; a-u) take; (D) inlay; (Š) instruct | 69
abūbu (n.) flood | 68
birītu (ii) (n.) fetter | 68
mamman (xp.) anybody; somebody | 68
maršītu (n.) property | 68
rē'ûtu (n.) shepherdship | 68
šaptu (n.) lip; crest | 68
tabrītu (n.) admiration; vision | 68
tanittu (n.) praise | 68
tuqumtu (n.) battle | 68
arba'u (nu.) four | 67
dāgilu (n.) one who obeys | 67
elēnu (av.) above; upstream of | 67
nikiltu (n.) cleverness; artful design | 67
še'û (v.; i) seek (out) | 67
agû (i) (n.) crown | 66
kadrû (n.) present | 66
labānu (v.; i) make bricks; stroke (the nose) | 66
rittu (n.) hand | 66
watmanu (n.) cella | 66
aššatu (n.) wife | 65
eperu (n.) earth; dirt; dust | 65
esēru (ii) (v.; i) enclose | 65
kīniš (av.) truly; reliably | 65
māmītu (n.) oath | 65
mukinnu (n.) one who firmly establishes, confirms | 65
rīmu (n.) wild bull | 65

Notes

List 5-D

Words Occurring 64–60 Times

askuppu (n.) (threshold) slab | 64
baḫūlātu (n.) men | 64
munakkiru (n.) one who alters something | 64
patru (n.) knife; sword | 64
ridûtu (n.) succession; successor | 64
eršu (iv) (n.) bed | 63
gitmālu (aj.) perfect | 63
kapādu (v.; u/i) plan | 63
pādû (aj.) forgiving | 63
purussû (n.) (legal) decision | 63
qanû (n.) reed | 63
šanû (iv) (v.; i) be(come) changed | 63
burāšu (n.) (species of) juniper | 62
diqāru (n.) large bowl | 62
ḫaṭû (v.; i) do wrong; be neglectful | 62
labāšu (v.; i) clothe oneself | 62
pulḫu (n.) terror | 62
tibku (n.) course of bricks | 62
ubānu (n.) finger; peak | 62
awīlūtu (n.) humanity | 61
karmu (n.) heap | 61
lē'û (aj.) competent; powerful | 61
misarru (n.) (metal) band | 61
awīlu (n.) man | 60
karšu (n.) stomach; mind | 60
kayyānu (aj.) constantly; regular | 60

Notes

List 5-E

Words Occurring 59–57 Times

aladlammû	(n.) human-headed bull-colossus | 59
eliš	(av.) above | 59
râmu (ii)	(v.; ā) love | 59
ṭābtu	(n.) goodness | 59
dumqu	(n.) goodness | 58
ekdu (i)	(aj.) wild; fierce | 58
ḫātu	(n.) terror | 58
māḫiru	(n.) opponent; recipient | 58
mīšaru	(n.) justice | 58
nāšû	(n.) bearer | 58
pāna	(av.) formerly | 58
qatû (ii)	(v.; i) finish; come to an end | 58
šapliš	(av.) below | 58
ummu (i)	(n.) mother | 58
waqru	(aj.) valuable | 58
wašbu	(aj.) inhabited; sitting | 58
abšānu	(n.) yoke | 57
edû (ii)	(v.; e) know | 57
ḫubtu	(n.) plunder; robbery | 57
nīšu (i)	(n.) lifting | 57
supû	(n.) prayer | 57
šadādu	(v.; a-u) drag | 57
šī	(ip.) she; that; this | 57
wasāmu	(v.; D) adorn; make fitting | 57

Notes

List 5-F

Words Occurring 56–52 Times

illatu	(n.) band; group | 56
inbu	(n.) fruit | 56
mazzāzu	(n.) position; one who is stationed | 56
nakliš	(av.) skillfully | 56
ummiānu	(n.) craftsman | 56
pašqu	(aj.) narrow; difficult | 55
ḫabātu (i)	(v.; a-u) loot; rob | 54
ḫerû	(v.; i) dig | 54
ulla (ii)	(av.) distant time; earliest times | 54
ḫengallu	(n.) plenty | 53
igāru	(n.) wall | 53
imēru (ii)	(n.) a unit of capacity | 53
karābu	(v.; a-u) bless; pray | 53
namrīru	(n.) awe-inspiring radiance | 53
nuḫšu	(n.) abundance | 53
rabîš	(av.) greatly; magnificently | 53
tidūku	(n.) battle; warrior | 53
gašru	(aj.) very strong | 52
katāmu	(v.; a-u) cover | 52
līpu	(n.) descendant | 52
ṣumbu	(n.) wagon | 52
šigaru	(n.) door lock; (neck-)stock | 52
šinni pīri	(n.) ivory | 52
ṭūbu	(n.) goodness | 52

Notes

List 5-G

Words Occurring 51–50 Times

kiššūtu (n.) exercise of power; authority | 51
qīpu (n.) delegate | 51
rēṣu (n.) helper | 51
šanû (iii) (v.; i) repeat; do twice | 51
šanû (i) (aj.) second; deputy | 51
tarbītu (n.) product of; rearing | 51
zaḫalû (n.) silver alloy | 51
akālu (v.; a-u) eat | 50
apālu (v.; a-u) answer; discuss | 50
aslu (ii) (n.) unit | 50
kūdanu (n.) mule | 50
magāru (v.; a-u) consent; accept | 50
malû (i) (aj.) full | 50
mašû (ii) (v.; i) forget | 50
rašādu (v.; Š) (Š) found; fasten securely | 50
šasû (v.; i) shout; call; read | 50
ziqqurratu (n.) ziggurat | 50

Notes

CHAPTER 6

Words Appearing Between 49 and 35 Times

Chapter 6 at a Glance	Total Number of Words in List	Total Number of Occurrences	Percentage of Occurrences in the Corpus
List 6-A: Words occurring 49–47 times	27	1,295	0.61%
List 6-B: Words occurring 46–44 times	25	1,135	0.53%
List 6-C: Words occurring 43–41 times	30	1,265	0.59%
List 6-D: Words occurring 40–39 times	32	1,260	0.59%
List 6-E: Words occurring 38–37 times	24	902	0.42%
List 6-F: Words occurring 36–35 times	28	993	0.46%
Total:	166	6,850	3.20%

Learning all the words in chapters 1–6 will enable you to read 88.62% of the words you encounter in Assyrian royal inscriptions.

List 6-A

Words Occurring 49–47 Times

abiktu	(n.) defeat | 49
gimillu	(n.) requital | 49
gimirtu	(n.) totality | 49
matīma	(av.) ever | 49
patāqu	(v.; i) cast; form (bricks) | 49
ruššû	(aj.) red | 49
šāninu	(n.) rival | 49
šunūti	(ip.) them; those | 49
û	(n.) grain | 49
arnu	(n.) guilt; punishment | 48
kisallu	(n.) courtyard | 48
nišītu	(n.) chosen one | 48
pašāḫu	(v.; a) be(come) at rest | 48
per'u	(n.) offspring | 48
sekretu	(n.) enclosed (woman) | 48
šâṭu (i)	(v.; ū) pull | 48
šurbû	(aj.) very great; very large | 48
ebūru	(n.) harvest; summer | 47
gipšu	(n.) massed body | 47
ḫidiātu	(n.) joy | 47
kimtu	(n.) family | 47
naprušu	(v.; N) fly | 47
rēštû	(aj.) foremost; firstborn | 47
rukūbu	(n.) vehicle; mount | 47
ša ēkalli	(n.) queen | 47
šakin māti	(n.) governor | 47
zā'eru	(n.) enemy | 47

Notes

List 6-B

Words Occurring 46–44 Times

akītu (n.) (cultic new year festival) | 46
erīšu (n.) scent | 46
ḫūdu (n.) happiness | 46
milku (n.) counsel; advice | 46
nāru (ii) (n.) musician | 46
nēšu (n.) lion | 46
paṭāru (v.; a-u) loosen; break up | 46
rakābu (v.; a) ride | 46
rakbû (n.) (mounted) messenger | 46
ṣarāpu (v.; a-u) burn; dye (red) | 46
šalḫû (n.) outer wall | 46
šapāku (v.; a-u) heap up | 46
šebû (v.; i) be satisfied; be(come) full | 46
ba'ūlātu (n.) subjects; people | 45
ḫišiḫtu (n.) requirement | 45
labīru (aj.) old | 45
ṣalmu (i) (aj.) black | 45
šalmiš (av.) in safety; well | 45
šaqû (ii) (v.; u) be(come) high | 45
šiknu (n.) appearance; act of putting | 45
zāwiānu (n.) enemy | 45
zâzu (v.; ū) dividc | 45
agammu (n.) marsh(es) | 44
dāriš (av.) forever | 44
mušaknišu (n.) one who makes someone submit | 44

Notes

List 6-C

Words Occurring 43–41 Times

abūbāniš	(av.) like a flood | 43
alālu (ii)	(v.; a-u) hang up | 43
ayyumma	(xp.) any; whoever | 43
barû (i)	(v.; i) inspect; search; perform divination | 43
erbu (ii)	(n.) sunset | 43
ḫarābu	(v.; u) be(come) deserted | 43
ḫašāḫu	(v.; a-u) desire | 43
mādiš	(av.) greatly; in large numbers | 43
muddišu	(n.) restorer | 43
niksu	(n.) cutting (off); breach | 43
sāpinu	(n.) flattener | 43
šākinu	(n.) one who places | 43
šuqultu	(n.) weight | 43
tillu	(n.) (military) equipment | 43
turminabandû	(n.) (a breccia or marble) | 43
argamannu	(n.) purple | 42
baṭlu	(aj.) ceased | 42
enû	(v.; i) change | 42
parāru	(v.; u) be broken up; (D) scatter | 42
šadālu	(v.; i) be(come) wide; (D) increase | 42
annu	(n.) yes | 41
appāru	(n.) marsh | 41
apsû	(n.) (cosmic) underground water | 41
dayyānu	(n.) judge | 41
ellāmu-	(prp.) before | 41
kuštāru	(n.) tent | 41
mitḫāriš	(av.) altogether; in the same manner | 41
mūdû	(aj.) knowing | 41
naparkû (i)	(aj.) ceasing | 41
ṣulūlu	(n.) roof; protection | 41

Notes

List 6-D

Words Occurring 40–39 Times

ādiru (n.) full of fear/awe | 40
daprānu (n.) juniper | 40
edû (i) (n.) wave | 40
ḫiṣbu (n.) abundance; yield | 40
ibilu (n.) camel | 40
mūṣû (n.) exit; escape route | 40
nâḫu (v.; ū) rest; become calm | 40
šâti (ip.) that | 40
šuātunu (ip.) those | 40
šuttu (n.) dream | 40
ṭuḫdu (n.) abundance | 40
urmaḫḫu (n.) lion colossus | 40
aggiš (av.) furiously | 39
apkallu (n.) sage | 39
attā (ip.) you | 39
igisû (n.) gift; contribution | 39
iḫzu (n.) mount; learning | 39
kidinnūtu (n.) tax-exempt status | 39
lišānu (n.) tongue; language | 39
līṭu (n.) hostage | 39
marratu (n.) sea | 39
muštarḫu (aj.) arrogant | 39
rīštu (n.) exultation | 39
salīmu (n.) peace | 39
sapāḫu (v.; a-u) scatter | 39
sīḫu (n.) rebellion | 39
šāru (i) (n.) wind; direction | 39
taḫtû (n.) defeat | 39
tartānu (n.) (high military official) | 39
tibûtu (n.) attack; swarm | 39
warkānu (av.) later | 39
zaqāru (v.; D) project; be high | 39

Notes

List 6-E

Words Occurring 38–37 Times

dabābu (ii)	(v.; u) speak | 38
dīnu	(n.) judgement; (legal) decision | 38
ḫurru	(n.) ravine | 38
kitnušu	(aj.) submissive | 38
kudurru (i)	(n.) labor obligation; carrying frame | 38
magal	(av.) very (much) | 38
maškanu	(n.) site; place | 38
nāmaru	(n.) watchtower | 38
nūnu	(n.) fish | 38
rupšu	(n.) width | 38
ṣimdu	(n.) yoke-team; fixed plan | 38
šalamtu	(n.) corpse | 38
tašriḫtu	(n.) glorification | 38
zunnu	(n.) rain | 38
bâ'u	(v.; ā) go along | 37
binûtu	(n.) creation; product | 37
ḫasīsu	(n.) wisdom; ear | 37
isinnu	(n.) festival | 37
mišiḫtu	(n.) dimension | 37
nābalu	(n.) dry land | 37
rēštu	(n.) first fruits; first rank | 37
šāt	(det.) that | 37
šeriktu	(n.) present | 37
tanattu	(n.) praise | 37

Notes

List 6-F

Words Occurring 36–35 Times

aplu (n.) heir | 36
eṭēru (v.; i) save; take away | 36
ḫasāsu (v.; a-u) be conscious about; plan | 36
māmū (n.) water | 36
nakru (i) (aj.) hostile; foreign | 36
namrāṣu (n.) hardship | 36
qilûtu (n.) burning | 36
sittūtu (n.) those remaining | 36
ṣābitu (n.) one who holds | 36
šār (nu.) 3600 | 36
šebēru (v.; i) break | 36
takiltu (n.) blue-purple (wool) | 36
ullû (dp.) distant; that | 36
ammiu (dp.) that | 35
ēdiš (av.) alone | 35
elēṣu (v.; i) rejoice | 35
gamāru (v.; a-u) finish; destroy | 35
kutallu (n.) behind; back | 35
litbušu (aj.) decorated; clothed | 35
maṣû (v.; i) achieve | 35
mušallimu (n.) deliverer; one who repays | 35
nūru (n.) light | 35
qarrādu (n.) warrior; hero | 35
qištu (n.) forest | 35
rebītu (n.) (town) square; district | 35
šapṣu (aj.) recalcitrant; difficult | 35
wēdu (aj.) single | 35
wussû (v.; D) identify; delineate | 35

Notes

CHAPTER 7

Words Appearing Between 34 and 26 Times

Chapter 7 at a Glance	Total Number of Words in List	Total Number of Occurrences	Percentage of Occurrences in the Corpus
List 7-A: Words occurring 34 times	16	544	0.25%
List 7-B: Words occurring 33 times	18	594	0.28%
List 7-C: Words occurring 32 times	16	512	0.24%
List 7-D: Words occurring 31 times	22	682	0.32%
List 7-E: Words occurring 30 times	19	570	0.27%
List 7-F: Words occurring 29 times	17	493	0.23%
List 7-G: Words occurring 28 times	21	588	0.27%
List 7-H: Words occurring 27 times	30	810	0.38%
List 7-I: Words occurring 26 times	20	520	0.24%
Total:	179	5,313	2.48%

Congratulations! Up to this point, you have learned nearly 90% of the words that you will encounter while reading Assyrian royal inscriptions. In chapters 7–9, you will be exposed to vocabulary that will enable you to recognize almost 95% of the words you will encounter in the corpus. As you familiarize yourselves with these words, consider reviewing the formation of the D and Š stems of verbs (cf. Huehnergard 2011, 252–336).

Remember that all D and Š stem verbs have an a-i vowel pattern, with the preterite and perfect sharing the same vowel (i). This pattern holds for the Dt, Dtn, Št, and Štn stems as well. Also, keep in mind that the only difference between the -t and -tn stems of the D and Š occurs in the durative. In all other forms, the Dtn is identical to the Dt and the Štn is identical to the Št. For more information on verbal vowel patterns, see appendix B.

List 7-A

Words Occurring 34 Times

ḫīrtu (n.) (equal ranking) wife
imbaru (n.) fog
išaru (aj.) righteous
kāru (n.) quay
kibsu (n.) route; track
kilallān (ip.) both
mēreḫtu (n.) insolence
nipḫu (n.) rising
pāqidu (n.) one who cares
paššuru (n.) dining tray; table
petû (i) (aj.) open
sūqu (n.) street
ṣeḫēru (v.; i) be(come) small
šiqlu (n.) shekel
šūquru (aj.) very valuable
šūturu (aj.) surpassing; very great

Notes

List 7-B

Words Occurring 33 Times

abarakkūtu	(n.) function of steward
aḫrītu	(n.) later time
bītānu	(n.) interior
buṭnu	(n.) terebinth
ḫuršāniš	(av.) like a mountain
liptu	(n.) undertaking; attack (of illness)
mušamqitu	(n.) one who cuts down
naṭālu	(v.; a-u) see; look
qabaltu	(n.) middle
qurdu	(n.) heroism
ṣalā'u	(v.; i) cast off
ṣīru (ii)	(n.) envoy
šamru	(aj.) furious
šaplu (ii)	(n.) beneath; bottom; underside
talīmu	(n.) (close or beloved) brother
terṣu	(n.) in the time of; pointing; protégé
ugāru	(n.) plain
zāninu	(n.) provisioner

Notes

List 7-C

Words Occurring 32 Times

akkullu	(n.) pick(axe); hatchet
arāru	(v.; a-u) curse
baṭālu	(v.; i) cease
bunnannû	(n.) (facial) features; physiognomy
karru (ii)	(n.) knob; peak; pommel
kašāṭu	(v.; i) cut down
kīam	(av.) so
mā	(prp.) saying
mušaklilu	(n.) completer
mušimmu	(n.) one who determines
pappardaliu	(n.) (a whitish semiprecious stone)
rigmu	(n.) sound; voice
riksu	(n.) structure; bond; contingent
sunqu	(n.) famine
tarāku	(v.; a-u) throb; (Š) make wield
ṭātu	(n.) bribe; gift

Notes

List 7-D

Words Occurring 31 Times

dāʾišu	(n.) crusher
kupru	(n.) bitumen
madbaru	(n.) desert; steppe
mukillu	(n.) holder
muqtablu	(n.) fighter
naparkû (ii)	(v.; N) cease; leave
natbāku	(n.) (mountain) gully
nēmedu	(n.) chair with back; socle
nēr	(nu.) | 600
rimītu	(n.) residence
ṣeḫru (ii)	(n.) childhood
šadlu	(aj.) broad; extensive
šangû	(n.) priest
šawiru	(n.) ring
šēdu	(n.) protective deity
šukkallu	(n.) vizier
tenēštu	(n.) people
urruḫiš	(av.) speedily
walādu	(v.; a-i) give birth
watû	(v.; a) find; (D) select
zaqru	(aj.) high; tall
zīmu	(n.) appearance; face

Notes

List 7-E

Words Occurring 30 Times

būlu	(n.) livestock; animals
dandannu	(aj.) all-powerful
elēnû	(aj.) upper
ēm	(prp.) wherever
enenna	(av.) now
itpēšu	(aj.) expert
kūnu	(n.) firmness
mušarbû	(n.) one who makes surpassing
mūtu	(n.) death
nigûtu	(n.) joyful song
pirištu	(n.) secret; specialized knowledge
qīštu	(n.) gift
re'û	(v.; e) shepherd
ṣurru (i)	(n.) obsidian
šaḫāṭu (ii)	(v.; a-u) tear off
šamāḫu	(v.; u) grow
šitmuru (i)	(aj.) very wild
šuklulu (i)	(aj.) completed; perfect
šumēla	(av.) on the left

Notes

List 7-F

Words Occurring 29 Times

dunnu	(n.) power
ištēniš	(av.) together; at the same time
kašāru	(v.; i) restore
mulmullu	(n.) arrow
murappišu	(n.) one who expands
nābû	(n.) one who calls by name
naḫallu	(n.) stream; gorge
nakālu	(v.; i) be(come) skillful
nēmequ	(n.) wisdom
rappu	(n.) (neck) stock
sulummû	(n.) peace-making
šalṭiš	(av.) imperiously
šaplānu	(av.) below; underneath
šibbu (i)	(n.) belt
ṭuppu	(n.) tablet
za'ānu	(v.; D) adorn
zību (i)	(n.) food offering

Notes

List 7-G

Words Occurring 28 Times

asaʾītu	(n.) pyramid; tower
birku	(n.) knee
dalālu	(v.; a-u) praise
durgu	(n.) innermost part; (royal) origin
gugallu	(n.) irrigation controller
ḫalāpu	(v.; u) slip into; be clothed
ḫušaḫḫu	(n.) need
isqu	(n.) lot; share
maṣṣartu	(n.) guard
munnabtu	(n.) fugitive
nārtu (ii)	(n.) female musician
nindanu	(n.) (a unit of measure)
qerû	(v.; i) invite
surrātu	(n.) lies
šalmu	(aj.) complete; favorable
šikaru	(n.) beer
šikittu	(n.) layout; form
ṭabtu	(n.) salt
uggatu	(n.) anger
unnīnu	(n.) prayer
wašṭu	(aj.) obdurate; stiff

Notes

List 7-H

Words Occurring 27 Times

aḫrâtaš	(av.) for ever after
apāru	(v.; i) put on the head
dullu	(n.) work
erēšu (ii)	(v.; i) request
eṣemtu	(n.) bone
etellu	(n.) pre-eminent one
gattu	(n.) form
ḫarīṣu	(n.) moat; ditch
ikkibu	(n.) taboo
kabāru (i)	(v.; i) be(come) thick
kummu	(n.) innermost room; cella
kuzbu	(n.) attractiveness
lapātu	(v.; a-u) touch; (Š) destroy
littūtu	(n.) old age
makāru	(v.; i) water; irrigate
mannu	(qp.) who?; whoever
mu'uddû	(n.) (large) quantity
mušabriqu	(n.) one who strikes with lightning
mušta''ûtu	(n.) leisure
nīšu (ii)	(n.) (oath on the) life
rēmēnû	(aj.) merciful
šaḫû	(n.) pig
šāpiru	(n.) leader; commander
šiāti	(ip.) that
ṭupšarru	(n.) scribe
udru	(n.) Bactrian camel
umāmu	(n.) animal
ūmišam	(av.) daily
usātu	(n.) help; assistance
waklu	(n.) overseer

Notes

List 7-I

Words Occurring 26 Times

adappu	(n.) horizontal crossbeam
allu	(n.) hoe
biri-	(prp.) among
burūmû	(n.) heaven
enšu	(aj.) weak; dilapidated
ḫabābu	(v.; u) gurgle; murmur
marāru	(v.; i) be bitter
mūrnisqu	(n.) war horse
muttabbilu	(n.) servant; one who maintains
nāgiru	(n.) herald
nekelmû	(v.; N) frown at
papāḫu	(n.) cella
šagāmu	(v.; u) roar
šurruḫu	(aj.) very proud
tabālu	(v.; a) take away
ṭēḫu	(n.) immediate vicinity
ṭūdu	(n.) path
uršānu	(n.) warrior
zanānu (i)	(v.; u) rain
zūku	(n.) infantry

Notes

CHAPTER 8

Words Appearing Between 25 and 20 Times

Chapter 8 at a Glance	Total Number of Words in List	Total Number of Occurrences	Percentage of Occurrences in the Corpus
List 8-A: Words occurring 25 times	20	500	0.23%
List 8-B: Words occurring 24 times	29	696	0.33%
List 8-C: Words occurring 23(a) times	21	483	0.23%
List 8-D: Words occurring 23(b) times	20	460	0.21%
List 8-E: Words occurring 22 times	27	594	0.28%
List 8-F: Words occurring 21(a) times	22	462	0.22%
List 8-G: Words occurring 21(b) times	20	420	0.20%
List 8-H: Words occurring 20 times	31	620	0.29%
Total:	190	4,235	1.98%

Chapters 7–9 will expose you to vocabulary that will enable you to recognize almost 95% of the words you will encounter in the corpus. As you familiarize yourselves with these words, consider reviewing the formation of middle-weak verbs in the G stem.

Remember: the vocal pattern of middle-weak verbs is determined by the nature of the "lost" consonant (ʾ/h → a; ʿ/ḥ → e; y → i; w → u). The G preterite will have a long vowel of the type associated with the lost consonant. The G perfect is based on the G preterite, with the characteristic infixed -t-. The G durative has an ultra-long vowel produced by contraction (long vowel + "a"), except in forms with a vocalic suffix, which have the appropriate short vowel followed by a doubled *final* radical (e.g., ikân, but ikunnū; iqīaš, but iqiššū) (cf. Huehnergard 2011, 67–68, 121–22, 182–83).

List 8-A

Words Occurring 25 Times

akalu (n.) bread; food
asurrû (n.) lower course
ba''ītu (n.) desired object
bāštu (n.) shame; dignity; genitalia
bēl narkabti (n.) charioteer
iltu (n.) goddess
imna (av.) on the right
kisirtu (n.) wall facing
lulû (n.) splendor
marû (i) (aj.) fattened
mērênu (n.) nakedness
namaddu (n.) darling
nasāku (v.; u) throw (down); (Š) remove
rebû (aj.) fourth
šalšu (aj.) third; one-third
šiltāḫu (n.) arrow
ṭābiš (av.) well
ušumgallu (n.) lion-dragon
wapû (v.; i) be(come) visible
waqāru (v.; i) be(come) valuable

Notes

List 8-B

Words Occurring 24 Times

akû	(n.) weak one
arītu	(n.) shield bearer; shield
bēru (i)	(aj.) distant
būrtu	(n.) well; cistern
gašīšu	(n.) stake
ḫilāni	(n.) portico
ištānu	(n.) north; north wind
ittu (i)	(n.) sign
kasû (iii)	(v.; i) bind
katāru	(v.; i) get (as) help
kulūlu	(n.) cornice
markasu	(n.) bond
marṣiš	(av.) laboriously
mātitān	(n.) (in) all lands
mukabbisu	(n.) one who treads on
nāmurtu	(n.) audience gift
našû (i)	(aj.) lifted; raised
pitqudu	(aj.) prudent; trustworthy
raḫāṣu (ii)	(v.; i/u) trust; (Š) give confidence
sāḫiru	(n.) searcher
sekret ēkalli	(n.) palace woman
sidru	(n.) row; battle line
šallu	(aj.) plundered
šapālu	(v.; i) be(come) deep
šeššu (ii)	(aj.) sixth; one-sixth
šīpātu	(n.) wool; cotton
šunu	(ip.) they; those
ṭeḫû	(v.; e) be(come) near
zakûtu	(n.) exemption

Notes

List 8-C

Words Occurring 23 Times (Part One)

aḫātu	(n.) sister
arammu	(n.) ramp
arku	(aj.) long
dalḫu	(aj.) disturbed; troubled
eršu (i)	(aj.) wise
ešmarû	(n.) (a silver alloy)
gišmaḫḫu	(n.) long beam
ḫibiltu	(n.) damage(s); wrongdoing
kakkabu	(n.) star
kasāru	(v.; i) pave
katmu	(aj.) covered; hidden
kirimaḫḫu	(n.) park
lā'iṭu	(n.) one who confines
māliku	(n.) adviser
mammāna	(xp.) who(so)ever
marqītu	(n.) refuge
masāku	(v.; Š) be(come) bad
muma''eru	(n.) commander; leader
nādinu	(n.) giver
nēbertu	(n.) opposite bank; crossing(-place)
nērārūtu	(n.) aid

Notes

List 8-D

Words Occurring 23 Times (Part Two)

nindabû	(n.) (food) offering
nudunnû	(n.) dowry
palkû	(aj.) broad
pašāqu	(v.; u) be(come) narrow
perku	(n.) transverse; region
rašubbatu	(n.) awesomeness
sugullu	(n.) herd
suppû	(v.; D) beseech
ṣabtu	(aj.) taken; seized
ṣāltu	(n.) combat
ṣīt šamši	(n.) sunrise
šaḫātu (iii)	(v.; u) be(come) afraid; revere
šašmu	(n.) (single) combat
šibirru	(n.) shepherd's staff
šipku	(n.) heap; pile
šukuttu	(n.) jewelry
šupšuqu	(aj.) very laborious
tibnu	(n.) straw
urbu	(n.) auxiliary force
warka	(av.) afterwards

Notes

List 8-E

Words Occurring 22 Times

anzillu	(n.) abomination
anzû	(n.) mythic storm-bird
appu	(n.) nose
azmarû	(n.) lance
ittu (ii)	(n.) sign
kamûtu	(n.) bondage
karmiš	(av.) into a ruin
kašūšu	(n.) (divine weapon)
kidinnu	(n.) protection
kunukku	(n.) seal
mêšu	(v.; ē) disregard; neglect
mušteʾʾû	(n.) assiduous one
nasāqu	(v.; a-u/i) choose
pasqu	(n.) coping (of a wall)
pattu	(n.) canal
qaqqariš	(av.) (down) to the ground
ṣerretu	(n.) nose-rope
ṣuḫḫuru (i)	(aj.) very small
ṣurru (ii)	(n.) heart; mind; interior
šamāmū	(n.) heavens
šatû (ii)	(v.; i) drink
šêlu	(v.; D) sharpen
šūpû	(aj.) resplendent
šūtu (ii)	(n.) south; south wind
yâši	(ip.) to me
ziqpu	(n.) pole; blade; shoot
zumru	(n.) body

Notes

List 8-F

Words Occurring 21 Times (Part One)

abāru (i)	(n.) (the metal) lead
alkakātu	(n.) actions; ways of life
ammar	(prp.) as much as
andullu	(n.) protection
balālu	(v.; a-u) mix (up)
bārtu	(n.) revolt
elāniš	(av.) above
elēlu (ii)	(v.; i) purify
enēšu	(v.; i) be(come) weak
epšu	(aj.) built; made
ezziš	(av.) furiously
ginû	(n.) regular offering
gullultu	(n.) sin
išippu	(n.) (a purification priest)
kâṣu	(v.; ū) flay
kimaḫḫu	(n.) grave
kurunnu	(n.) (a kind of beer)
maḫīru	(n.) market price; trade
meḫû	(n.) storm
mula''iṭu	(n.) one who encircles
muribbu	(n.) one who makes tremble
mušēribu	(n.) one who brings in

Notes

List 8-G

Words Occurring 21 Times (Part Two)

muterru	(n.) (re)turner
mutnennû	(aj.) pious
muttaprišu	(aj.) flying; winged
nablu (i)	(n.) flame; flash
naklu	(aj.) skillful
namṣāru	(n.) sword
nannāru	(n.) moon; light
parāʾu	(v.; a-u) cut through
serdu	(n.) olive tree
ṣūmu	(n.) thirst
šadāḫu	(v.; i) march; pass along
šaniānu	(av.) (for the) second time
šâšunu	(ip.) them
šurrû (i)	(n.) beginning
šūt (iii)	(prp.) because of; concerning
tappûtu	(n.) assistance
teknû	(n.) comfort; praise
têrtu	(n.) instruction; omen
ṭabāḫu	(v.; a-u) slaughter
ullânu	(av.) before

Notes

List 8-H

Words Occurring 20 Times

agāgu	(v.; a-u) be(come) furious
arratu	(n.) curse
balu	(prp.) without
banû (i)	(aj.) beautiful; good
bitrû (ii)	(v.; i) endure
dimtu (i)	(n.) tower
dišpu	(n.) honey
erbû	(n.) locust
erû (i)	(n.) eagle
ḫamṭiš	(av.) quickly
ḫassu	(aj.) wise; clever
ilku	(n.) corvée (tax labor)
kamîš	(av.) in a bound state
lalû	(n.) charms
malāku	(v.; i) advise; discuss
miṭirtu	(n.) watercourse
muštaḫṭu	(n.) escapee
nasīku	(n.) tribal leader
nawû (i)	(n.) pasturage; steppe
nēḫtu	(n.) calm
pītu	(n.) opening
raggu	(n.) wicked person
ṣarpu (i)	(aj.) dyed; baked
ṣibittu	(n.) captivity
ṣītān	(av.) in the east
šaḫtu	(aj.) reverent
šarḫu	(aj.) proud; splendid
šīlān	(av.) in the west
tālittu	(n.) offspring
taqānu	(v.; u) be(come) secure; be in good order
zikrūtu	(n.) manliness

Notes

CHAPTER 9

Words Appearing Between 19 and 15 Times

Chapter 9 at a Glance	**Total Number of Words in List**	**Total Number of Occurrences**	**Percentage of Occurrences in the Corpus**
List 9-A: Words occurring 19 times	27	513	0.24%
List 9-B: Words occurring 18(a) times	20	360	0.17%
List 9-C: Words occurring 18(b) times	20	360	0.17%
List 9-D: Words occurring 17(a) times	22	374	0.17%
List 9-E: Words occurring 17(b) times	21	357	0.17%
List 9-F: Words occurring 16(a) times	23	368	0.17%
List 9-G: Words occurring 16(b) times	24	384	0.18%
List 9-H: Words occurring 15(a) times	25	375	0.18%
List 9-I: Words occurring 15(b) times	25	375	0.18%
Total:	207	3,466	1.62%

Chapters 7–9 will expose you to vocabulary that will enable you to recognize almost 95% of the words you will encounter in the corpus. As you familiarize yourselves with these words, consider reviewing the formation of I-weak verbs (I-a/e, I-n, I-w) in the G and N stems.

Remember: I-weak verbs are largely regular in the G durative, as long as you remember that I-w verbs begin with a u-vowel instead of *iwa-. For I-a/e verbs, the G preterite and perfect both have lengthened prefix vowels (cf. Huehnergard 2011, 54–55, 168). For I-n verbs, the "n" assimilates to the middle root letter in the G preterite and to the infixed -t- of the perfect (Huehnergard 2011, 155–56). For I-w verbs, the G perfect behaves as though the word were a I-n (Huehnergard 2011, 182–83). In all tenses of the N stem, I-a/e verbs behave as though they were I-n verbs (Huehnergard 2011, 376).

List 9-A

Words Occurring 19 Times

alaktu	(n.) way; course
apu	(n.) reed-bed; reeds
arāḫu	(v.; a) hasten; (D) send speedily
bâru (i)	(v.; ā) catch
berqu	(n.) lightning
dabābu (i)	(n.) talk; speech
ditalliš	(av.) into ashes
egalturrû	(n.) little palace
guḫlu	(n.) antimony (paste)
ḫurbāšu	(n.) terror
kamāsu (ii)	(v.; i) kneel
kiṣṣu	(n.) shrine
mār šipri	(n.) messenger
mašqītu	(n.) watering place
napāḫu	(v.; a-u) rise; ignite
pašālu	(v.; i) crawl
piqittu	(n.) post; provisions
qarrādūtu	(n.) heroism
rabāṣu	(v.; i) sit; crouch
šandabakku	(n.) chief accountant
šanûti-	(av.) for the second time
šitūltu	(n.) discussion
ṭebû	(v.; u) sink
uṣurtu	(n.) design; ground-plan
watartu	(n.) addition
wu''urtu	(n.) command
yašibu	(n.) battering-ram

Notes

List 9-B

Words Occurring 18 Times (Part One)

agû (ii)	(n.) flood
bābilu	(n.) one who carries
ebertu	(n.) bank
ešqu	(aj.) massive
ezēzu	(v.; i) be(come) angry
gallû	(n.) (a demon)
ḫibištu	(n.) crushed pieces (of aromatics)
ḫimētu	(n.) ghee
kiškattû (ii)	(n.) craftsman
labīrūtu	(n.) old age
lamādu	(v.; a) learn
maʾdû	(n.) (large) quantity
maruštu	(n.) evil
māšartu	(n.) review
muparriru	(n.) one who scatters
muštēširu	(n.) one who sets straight
nâdu (i)	(v.; ā) praise
nebrītu	(n.) hunger
nītu	(n.) encirclement
pašallu	(n.) (gold alloy)

Notes

List 9-C

Words Occurring 18 Times (Part Two)

râbu	(v.; ū) tremble
sadāru	(v.; i) put in order; do regularly
sanāqu	(v.; i) check; approach
suluppu	(n.) date
ṣabītu	(n.) gazelle
ṣarāḫu (iii)	(v.; a-u) heat up; become angry
ṣummirātu	(n.) desires
šalummatu	(n.) radiance
šaqû (iii)	(v.; i) give to drink; irrigate
šiāḫu	(v.; ī) grow (tall)
tallaktu	(n.) passage; walkway
tarānu	(n.) roof
tiālu	(n.) white cedar
titūru	(n.) bridge; aqueduct
ṭarādu	(v.; a-u) drive away; send away
ūṣu	(n.) arrow
zaʾnu	(aj.) adorned
zabbilu	(n.) bearer
zaqtu	(aj.) pointed
zayyāru	(n.) foe

Notes

List 9-D

Words Occurring 17 Times (Part One)

adnātu	(n.) world; people
andurāru	(n.) exemption; freedom
asliš	(av.) like sheep
bārû	(n.) diviner
bu''uru	(n.) hunting
būnu	(n.) face; outward appearance
daqāqu	(v.; D) crush
dūru (ii)	(n.) permanence; eternity
emqu	(aj.) wise; skilled
ešītu	(n.) (political) disorder
gabarû	(n.) copy; opponent
gišḫurru	(n.) design; plan
ḫalṣu	(n.) fortress
ḫamṭu	(aj.) quick
ḫitlupu	(aj.) clad in; intertwined
ḫiṭītu	(n.) crime
ḫurrušu	(aj.) bound
kippatu	(n.) perimeter; ring; circle
kuppu	(n.) water-source
lābu	(n.) lion
mâdu	(v.; ī) make numerous
mušītu	(n.) night(-time)

Notes

List 9-E

Words Occurring 17 Times (Part Two)

nizmatu	(n.) desire
parāku	(v.; i) block; contravene
pendû	(n.) (a semiprecious reddish stone)
puzru	(n.) hidden place; refuge
qarānu	(v.; a-u) stack up
qarnu	(n.) horn
qû (i)	(n.) thread; web
rubûtu	(n.) prince-ship
ṣillu	(n.) shade; protection
šadû (ii)	(n.) east
šalû (ii)	(v.; u) cast away; shoot
šammu	(n.) plant(s)
šipṭu (i)	(n.) judgement
šubarrû	(n.) (tax) exemption
tamlītu	(n.) filling; inlay (of stones)
urpatu	(n.) cloud
ušallu	(n.) lowland; river-flats
utullu	(n.) herdsman
wālidu	(n.) one who begets
warḫišamma	(av.) monthly
zabālu	(v.; i) carry

Notes

List 9-F

Words Occurring 16 times (Part One)

abbūtu	(n.) fatherhood
awû	(v.; u) speak
bu'āru	(n.) good fortune
ēdēnu	(av.) alone
ernittu	(n.) triumph
eṣēru	(v.; i) draw; design
gerû	(v.; i) be(come) hostile
gillatu	(n.) sin
ḫarru	(n.) water channel
kalbu	(n.) dog
kappu (ii)	(n.) (small) bowl; hand
kaškaššu	(n.) all-powerful one
kerḫu	(n.) citadel; enclosed area
kidudû	(n.) rites
kigallu	(n.) pedestal; socle; netherworld
kūm	(prp.) instead of
kūṣu	(n.) coldness; winter
manāma	(xp.) somebody; who(so)ever
māraku	(n.) full extent; length
mašû (i)	(aj.) forgotten
mayyālu	(n.) bed
minûtu	(n.) count(ing); number
nadru	(aj.) raging

Notes

List 9-G

Words Occurring 16 Times (Part Two)

nakkamtu	(n.) treasure
namkūru	(n.) property
napāšu	(v.; u) breath; (N) relax
nārtu (i)	(n.) canal; river
nesû (i)	(aj.) distant; far
pagû	(n.) monkey
pārisu	(n.) one who decides
pīḫātūtu	(n.) governorship
pilšu	(n.) breach
rāḫiṣu	(n.) one who devastates
rîtu	(n.) pasture
sellu	(n.) arch
siāqu	(v.; ī) reduce
sidirtu	(n.) line of battle
ṣalālu	(v.; a) lie (down); sleep
šāgišu	(n.) murderer
šaḫūru (i)	(n.) (part of a temple); cultic 'summit building'
šibṭu	(n.) plague
šupku	(n.) foundation
šūt (ii)	(ip.) he; it; that (one)
tapḫu	(n.) (a metal cauldron)
tikpu (ii)	(n.) brick course
urigallu	(n.) divine standard
wālittu	(n.) one who gives birth

Notes

List 9-H

Words Occurring 15 Times (Part One)

abbu	(n.) swamp
alamittu	(n.) (a wild species of date palm)
anantu	(n.) battle
anāqāte	(n.) she-camels
appātu	(n.) portico
bitrû (i)	(aj.) prime quality; enormous
bubūtu (i)	(n.) hunger; starvation
dārišam	(av.) forever
ḫabālu	(v.; i) do wrong
iṣṣūriš	(av.) like a bird
kabābu (i)	(n.) shield
kalû (iii)	(n.) lamentation-priest
kapru	(n.) village
karû (ii)	(v.; i) be(come) short
kāṣiru	(n.) one who arranges
kīmū	(prp.) instead of
kullu (iii)	(v.; D) hold
maqittu	(n.) dilapidation
maštaku	(n.) chamber
mītūtu	(n.) (state of) death
muḫḫurtu	(n.) facing (side); opposite (side)
munarriṭu	(n.) one who makes tremble
mušlālu	(n.) staircase(-gate)
naptanu	(n.) banquet; meal(-time)
nēbeḫu	(n.) frieze

Notes

List 9-I

Words Occurring 15 Times (Part Two)

nêšakku	(n.) (a dignitary)
pānātu	(n.) front part; prior time
paramāḫu	(n.) throne dais
pelludû	(n.) ritual
qâpu	(v.; ū) fall down
qīšu	(n.) forest
quppu	(n.) cage
qurpissu	(n.) helmet
rabbû	(aj.) large
rēḫtu	(n.) remainder
ṣaliptu	(n.) lying
ṣēnu (i)	(n.) evil (one)
šabāsu	(v.; u) be(come) angry
šalāšī-	(av.) for the third time; three times
šālilu	(n.) plunderer
šalšāya	(n.) third brother
šapšāqu	(n.) hardship; constraint
šû	(n.) sheep
šurīnu	(n.) (divine) emblem
tēmīqu	(n.) prayer
terḫatu	(n.) dowry
teslītu	(n.) petition; request
ulṣu	(n.) pleasure
urru	(n.) day
zuqtu	(n.) mountain peak

Notes

CHAPTER 10

Words Appearing Between 14 and 5 Times

Chapter 10 at a Glance	Total Number of Words in List	Total Number of Occurrences	Percentage of Occurrences in the Corpus
List 10: Words occurring 14–5 times	958	8,102	3.79%

If you learn all of the vocabulary in chapters 1–10, you will be able to recognize nearly 99% of the words you encounter in Assyrian royal inscriptions. However, it is unlikely that you will be able to memorize all of the words in this final chapter. Instead, you should use the following lists to supplement your review of earlier chapters. That is, as you go back through this book to test your memorization of the lists in chapters 1–9, consider adding in a handful of words from one of the lists in chapter 10 to further fortify your vocabulary. If you wish to have information regarding words that occur fewer than 5 times, consult appendix H.

List 10

14 Occurrences

abāku (i)	(v.; a-u) lead away
amurru	(n.) west
atwû	(n.) speech
barāqu	(v.; i) strike with lightning
bašāmu (ii)	(v.; i) create
erḫu	(aj.) aggressive
gabbu	(n.) totality
gumāḫu	(n.) prize bull
ḫamšu	(aj.) fifth
igirû	(n.) heron
inūšu	(av.) at that time
iššiakkūtu	(n.) ensi-ship
lānu	(n.) form; size
lētu	(n.) cheek
maḫrû (iii)	(av.) previously
maqlūtu	(n.) burn(ing)
māšu	(aj.) twin
mazzaztu	(n.) position
miqtu	(n.) fall
muʾabbitu	(n.) destroyer
mūlû	(n.) ascent
mumtalku	(aj.) circumspect
munawwiru	(aj.) brightening
musappiḫu	(n.) scatterer
mušpalu	(n.) depth
muttarrû	(n.) leader
nāʾeru	(aj.) roaring
nabāsu	(n.) red wool
nagāšu	(v.; u) wander about
naḫarmuṭu	(v.; Š) dissolve
nannābu	(n.) offspring
napāṣu	(v.; a-u) smash
nasqu	(aj.) chosen
naṭû	(aj.) suited
nummuru	(aj.) very bright
piriggallu	(n.) lion colossus
qalû (ii)	(v.; i) burn

riḫṣu	(n.) flood(ing)
samānû	(aj.) eighth
ṣerru (i)	(n.) snake
šamāru	(i) (v.; u) rage
šâmu	(v.; ā) buy
šapku	(aj.) heaped up
šeššu (i)	(nu.) six
šitrāḫu	(aj.) very proud
šuršu	(n.) root
šutāḫû	(aj.) matching
tašīmtu	(n.) discernment
tīru	(n.) courtier
tizqāru	(aj.) supreme
ṭīdu	(n.) clay
uḫḫuzu	(aj.) overlaid
urigallu	(n.) divine standard
utūnu	(n.) kiln
uṭṭatu	(n.) grain (food or unit)
zēru (i)	(aj.) hostile

13 Occurrences

adānu	(n.) appointed time
arbūtu	(n.) barren land; desolation
bakru	(n.) foal
bamātu	(n.) open country
batūlu	(n.) boy
butuqtu	(n.) breach
dābibu	(n.) one who speaks
danniš	(av.) very
diānu	(v.; ī) judge
ela	(prp.) apart from
eššu	(aj.) new
gāmilu	(aj.) merciful
ḫepû (ii)	(v.; i) break; destroy
ḫiāṭu	(v.; ī) inspect; seek out
ḫīpu	(n.) break(age)
išariš	(av.) correctly; normally
kaqdâ	(av.) constantly
laḫmu	(n.) a mythical being
laplaptu	(n.) thirst

lemēnu	(v.; i) be(come) bad
madaktu	(n.) (military) camp
malmališ	(av.) equally
maṣṣaru	(n.) guard
mašāḫu	(v.; a-u) measure
mašqû	(n.) watering place
minītu	(n.) limbs; measure
mitgāru	(aj.) favorable
mitḫurtu	(n.) convergence
nadāru	(v.; N) be(come) wild
nalbanu	(n.) brick mold
nāsiḫu	(n.) one who removes
natāru	(v.; Š) hack out
papallu	(n.) young shoot
parūtu	(n.) (a type of alabaster)
pirṣātu	(n.) lies
puqqu	(v.; D) be anxious; heed
qallu	(aj.) light; little
qardūtu	(n.) heroism; warriorhood
riābu	(v.; ī) replace; compensate
rūštu	(n.) (a fine quality of oil)
sāmtu	(n.) carnelian; dawn
seḫû	(v.; i) rise up; revolt
serrēmu	(n.) onager
ṣalî	(aj.) situated
ṣarāšu	(v.; D) spread out
ṣāriru	(n.) (a gold alloy)
ṣubātu	(n.) garment; textile
ṣubbû	(v.; D) inspect
šagāšu	(v.; i) murder
šamāmiš	(av.) to heaven
šināti	(ip.) them; those
šinīšu	(av.) in two; twice
šumēlu	(n.) the left
šurbûtu	(aj.) very great; supreme
šuršudu	(aj.) firmly founded
tarbaṣu	(n.) courtyard; enclosure
tarpašû	(n.) area
tašīltu	(n.) festivity; joy
uzzu	(n.) anger
wadû	(v.; D) know; (D) allocate; identify

wēdiššī-	(av.) he/you (etc.) alone
zāninūtu	(n.) role of provisioner
zāratu	(n.) tent
ziāqu	(v.; ī) blow

12 Occurrences

aḫû	(aj.) foreign(er)
akāmu	(n.) dust-cloud
alallu	(n.) (a stone)
arḫiš	(av.) quickly
birtūtu	(n.) fortification
dāru	(n.) era; eternity
dikuggallu	(n.) chief justice
duššupu	(aj.) sweetened; very sweet
elammakku	(n.) (a tree); (a valuable wood)
erbêšu	(av.) for the fourth time; four times
eṣru	(aj.) designed; drawn
gupnu	(n.) tree(-trunk)
ḫammāʾu	(n.) rebel; usurper
ḫissatu	(n.) mention; understanding
ḫittu	(n.) lintel
ḫuššû	(aj.) red
ibrūtu	(n.) friendship
iḫzētu	(n.) decorative inlay
ilittu	(n.) birth; offspring
inanna	(av.) now
kābisu	(n.) one who treads on
kummuru	(aj.) loaded; piled up
lābiš	(av.) like a lion
magarru	(n.) wagon; wheel
mēlû	(n.) high place; step
mīnu (i)	(qp.) what?
murṣu	(n.) illness
naʾādu	(v.; i) be(come) attentive
nābiʾu	(n.) plunderer
nabû (i)	(aj.) called; named
nakmu	(aj.) heaped (up)
nammušīšu	(n.) death
qerītu	(n.) banquet
raksu (i)	(aj.) joined; tied; tight

rašbu (aj.) awe-inspiring
rīmāniš (av.) like a wild bull
ru'āmu (n.) love; lovemaking
saḫālu (v.; a-u) pierce
saḫliu (n.) cress
salātu (ii) (v.; a) slice through; slit
sapannu (n.) plain
sipittu (n.) mourning (rites)
ṣiṣṣu (n.) (a wooden bar?)
šaddû'a (n.) mountain-dweller
šêtu (v.; ē/ī) be remaining
šībūtu (n.) old age; testimony
šillatu (n.) impudence; iniquity
šūluku (aj.) befitting; appropriate
šurrâtu (n.) start
tāmiḫu (n.) one who grasps
targīgu (n.) evildoer
ṭupšarrūtu (n.) scribal learning
upnu (n.) hollow of the hand
urudû (n.) copper
zanānu (ii) (v.; a-u) provide

11 Occurrences

aḫennâ (av.) each by it/himself
āḫizu (n.) informed person
aḫurrû (n.) social inferior
Anūtu (n.) Anu-ship (i.e. akin to Anu)
ašlu (n.) unit
attū- (ip.) belonging to
baqāmu (v.; a-u) pluck
bārānû (n.) rebel
bašû (ii) (aj.) existing
batultu (n.) young girl
bērūtu (n.) mound
bu''û (v.; D) look for
bukru (n.) son
dikûtu (n.) levy
dimtu (ii) (n.) tear
dušû (n.) rafts of (inflated) skins
esēqu (v.; i) carve; incise

ḫamâtu	(n.) help
ḫanābu	(v.; u) make grow luxuriantly
išpatu	(n.) quiver
itūlu	(v.; ī) (make) lie down
itûtu	(n.) selection
kīlu	(n.) prison
kinūnu	(n.) brazier; oven
kisû	(n.) area around base of building
kišubbû	(n.) waste ground
maḫḫû	(n.) ecstatic
mašrû	(n.) riches
meḫru (i)	(n.) copy; equivalent
mešrêtu	(n.) limbs
mīšariš	(av.) in justice
mušapšiḫu	(n.) one who pacifies
mušēzibu	(n.) one who saves oneself
muššāru	(n.) (serpentine stone)
muštālu	(n.) circumspect one
nābališ	(av.) into/on dry land
nanzuzu	(aj.) was standing
naquttu	(n.) (state of) distress
narāṭu	(v.; u) tremble
narbāṣu	(n.) lair (of an animal)
nērtu	(n.) murder
nêru (ii)	(n.) killer
nidûtu	(n.) waste land; abandonment
nussuqu	(aj.) choice
palḫiš	(av.) fearfully; reverently
pargāniš	(av.) in security
qarītu	(n.) grain-store
radādu	(v.; a-u) drive away; pursue
sapḫu	(aj.) scattered
ṣibtu (i)	(n.) seizure
šabburtu	(n.) cultivated land
šaḫāṭu (i)	(v.; i) jump (on); attack
šamriš	(av.) furiously
šitimgallu	(n.) master builder
šuplu	(n.) depth
takkassu	(n.) unworked block
taklu	(aj.) trusted
tardennu	(aj.) second

tūʾamu	(n.) twin; double door
ṭāridu	(n.) one who drives away
uḫummiš	(av.) like a cliff
waṣābu	(v.; a-i) add; increase
zaqīpu	(n.) stake
ziqnu	(n.) beard

10 Occurrences

aḫannâ	(av.) on this bank
āmiru	(n.) one who sees
asmiš	(av.) in a fitting manner
asu	(n.) bear
asurrakku	(n.) water below ground; depths
ašnan	(n.) grain
ayyalu	(n.) stag
baltu	(n.) (a spiny plant)
barakku	(n.) (a corridor)
buqlu	(n.) malt
dalû	(n.) bucket
diāšu	(v.; ī) trample; tread down
dilûtu	(n.) bucket
dunnunu	(aj.) very strong
eblu	(n.) cord; rope
epinnu	(n.) plough; (a constellation)
ereqqu	(n.) cart
ermu	(n.) cover(ing)
eṣēdu (ii)	(v.; i) harvest
gisallû	(n.) eaves
gišimmaru	(n.) date palm
ḫābilu	(n.) criminal
ḫabû	(v.; u) draw (water)
ḫâlu	(v.; ī) melt (away)
ḫaṣbattu	(n.) (a pottery bowl)
imnu	(n.) right (side)
isāru	(n.) (part of the temple complex)
iṣratu	(n.) ground-plan
izqātu	(n.) fetters
kalbānātu	(n.) (a siege instrument)
kallātu	(n.) daughter-in-law
kāmû	(n.) one who binds

kamû (i)	(aj.) bound (one); prisoner
kannu	(n.) pedestal; stand
lēqû	(n.) one who takes
lumnu	(n.) evil
lurmu	(n.) ostrich
mānaḫtu	(n.) fatigue; weariness
maqtu	(aj.) fallen; collapsed
mētellūtu	(n.) rulership
mimmû	(xp.) all that; whatever
miqittu	(n.) collapse
muneḫḫu	(n.) one who repulses
munêru	(n.) one who strikes
mupattû	(n.) one who opens
murteddû	(n.) one who controls
mūtānu	(n.) epidemic
nabāṭu	(v.; u) make shine
nakriš	(av.) like an enemy
namba'u	(n.) source
narbâtu	(n.) end(ing)
nēmettu	(n.) couch
niṭlu	(n.) appearance; gaze; look
pašāru	(v.; a-u) forgive; sell
pattiš	(av.) like a canal
pušqu	(n.) distress; narrow pass
qablû	(aj.) central
qerbetu	(n.) meadowland
qutru	(n.) smoke
raḫāṣu (i)	(v.; i) flood; devastate
rukkusu	(aj.) harnessed
salḫu	(aj.) sprinkled
sāniqu	(n.) controller
saplu	(n.) bowl
sebû	(aj.) seventh
seḫru	(n.) all; region; turn
sippu	(n.) (door-)jamb; buttress
suḫḫurtu	(n.) retreat
ṣaddu	(n.) portent
ṣullulu (ii)	(v.; D) roof over
ṣumāmu	(n.) thirst
ṣuṣû	(n.) reed-thicket
šaggaštu	(n.) murder; slaughter

šagigurrû	(n.) free-will offering
šanîš	(av.) ditto
šaqummatu	(n.) (deathly) hush
šâša	(ip.) that; to her
šēṭūtu	(n.) scorn
šuluḫḫu	(n.) purification rite
šuribatu	(n.) terror?
tabku	(aj.) spilled; stored
taqrubtu	(n.) battle
tašlīšu	(n.) third man (on a chariot)
tikku	(n.) nape of the neck
tillatu	(n.) auxiliaries
udû	(n.) container; equipment
waqû	(v.; i) wait (for)
wāšipu	(n.) exorcist; incantation priest
ziqtu	(n.) (a disease); peak; point

9 Occurrences

aburriš	(av.) in a green pasture
adanniš	(av.) greatly
agappu	(n.) wing
ambassu	(n.) (game-)park
anḫu	(aj.) tired; dilapidated
aslu (i)	(n.) ram
ašāgu	(n.) (a common spiny plant)
ašgigû	(n.) (a mineral)
āširu	(n.) inspector
ašūḫu	(n.) pine-tree
attī	(ip.) you
babālu	(v.; a-i) carry
bīru	(n.) divination
būru (ii)	(n.) (bull) calf
būru (iv)	(n.) hunger
burzigallu	(n.) (a big vessel)
egerrû	(n.) ominous utterance
erbu (i)	(n.) income
ḫadû (iii)	(v.; u) be(come) joyful
ḫamāṭu (ii)	(v.; u) hasten
ḫarḫarru	(n.) chain
ḫašādu	(n.) wedding

ḫašūru	(n.) (a kind of cypress)
ḫerṣu	(n.) image; form
ḫiāšu	(v.; ī) hurry
ḫitmuṭiš	(av.) very quickly
ḫūlu	(n.) way
imtu	(n.) poison
kalakku	(n.) (a kind of wall-plaster)
kallāpu	(n.) (a foot-soldier)
kāpu	(n.) cliff
kaṣû	(aj.) cold
kisittu	(n.) ancestry; branches
kisurrû	(n.) boundary; territory
kurkû	(n.) goose
lalgar	(n.) cosmic (underground) water
lulīmu	(n.) stag
maḫḫūtiš	(av.) like a female ecstatic
masabbu	(n.) (a basket)
mēteqtu	(n.) advance
mitḫuṣūtu	(n.) battle
mūru	(n.) young animal
mušaššiku	(n.) one who abolishes
naburru	(n.) battlement
nādu (i)	(n.) (water-)skin
narāmtu	(n.) beloved (woman)
nēberu	(n.) crossing point
palāqu	(v.; i) slaughter
palgu	(n.) canal
paqdu	(aj.) entrusted
pātiqu	(n.) one who fashions
piātu	(n.) edge
qanānu	(v.; a-u) make a nest
qu''û	(v.; D) await
ramû (iii)	(v.; u) be(come) loose
rašubbu	(aj.) awesome
saḫmaštu	(n.) rebellion
salmu	(aj.) friendly; propitious
sāmu	(aj.) red
sapāru	(n.) (deity's) net
sariyam	(n.) armor
sartu	(n.) falsehood
sekēru	(v.; i) block up

sikiptu	(n.) repulse
simmiltu	(n.) siege-ladder; staircase
sindû	(n.) (a type of wood)
ṣamāru	(v.; D) strive for; wish for
šâʾu	(v.; ū) fly
šalāpu	(v.; a-u) pull out
šalgu	(n.) snow
šallūtu	(n.) state of captivity
šāriku	(n.) one who presents (gifts)
šēmû	(n.) one who hears
šēru (ii)	(n.) morning
šuglutu	(aj.) awe-inspiring; very frightening
šūpušu	(aj.) built; completed
šuqallulu	(aj.) hanging
šutābulu	(aj.) mixed; deliberating
tākultu	(n.) meal
tamû	(v.; a) swear (an oath)
tappû	(n.) partner
tarlugallu	(n.) rooster
tašrītu	(n.) inauguration
tēnû	(n.) replacement
tilpānu	(n.) bow
tullû	(aj.) bedecked
ummânūtu	(n.) scribal craft; craftsmanship
urqītu	(n.) vegetation
wuṣṣû	(v.; D) present (a dedicatory offering)
zamû	(n.) outer corner
zuqiqīpu	(n.) scorpion

8 Occurrences

abtu	(aj.) destroyed
agālu	(n.) donkey
aggu	(aj.) furious
allāku	(n.) messenger
āpiru	(n.) crowned one
appatu	(n.) rein
armu	(n.) mountain goat
ayyakku	(n.) (a type of sanctuary)
bārûtu	(n.) work of the diviner
bussurtu	(n.) message

dapīnu	(aj.) savage; overbearing
dīku	(aj.) killed
duruššu	(n.) foundation (platform)
ebēbu	(v.; i) cleanse
elītu	(n.) above; upper world
Ellilūtu	(n.) power of Enlil
ēribu	(n.) enterer
eššēšu	(n.) (a feast day)
galātu	(v.; u) tremble; make tremble
gallu	(aj.) rolling
gamālu	(v.; i) be obliging; spare
gapāšu	(v.; u) be(come) swollen
gipāru	(n.) pastureland
guḫaššu	(n.) wire
ḫā'iṭu	(n.) watcher
ḫadû (ii)	(n.) joy
ḫalluptu	(n.) armor
ḫamāṭu (iii)	(v.; a-u) burn (up)
ḫarāṣu	(v.; a-u) excavate; reduce
ḫatānu	(v.; i) protect
ḫuḫāriš	(av.) as with a bird-snare
igulû	(n.) fine ointment
kādu	(n.) guard
kalappu	(n.) pickaxe
kamāru (ii)	(n.) defeat
kamru	(aj.) piled up
kamû (ii)	(v.; i) capture
karû (i)	(n.) (grain)heap
kirimmu	(n.) (crook of) arm
kubru	(n.) thickness; diameter
kumû	(n.) (a water bird)
kupû	(n.) reed thicket
kušīru	(n.) success
lābinu	(n.) brick-maker; one who strokes (the nose)
lâṭu	(v.; ū) encircle; keep in check
līliātu	(n.) evening
maḫra	(av.) before; in front
makutu	(n.) pole
malikūtu	(n.) rulership
marru (ii)	(n.) shovel
maštītu	(n.) (allowance of) drink

mēsū	(n.) rites
mubbibu	(n.) purifier
muḫḫuṣu	(aj.) hurt
muniḫḫu (i)	(n.) one who overpowers
mūraku	(n.) length
mušammiḫu	(n.) one who makes flourish
mušamṣû	(n.) one who brings out
mušēšeru	(n.) one who puts in order
nakādu	(v.; u) be anxious
nakāpu (i)	(v.; i) abut; battle
namûtu	(n.) wasteland
napardû (ii)	(v.; N) lighten; shine brightly
napardû (i)	(aj.) shining brightly
našpartu	(n.) message
nēpeštu	(n.) work
neqelpû	(v.; N) sail
palāku	(v.; a-u) demarcate
pašḫu	(n.) (a hand-held weapon)
pilku (i)	(n.) boundary
pitnu	(n.) chest
pulukku	(n.) boundary (marker)
qannu	(n.) border
qiššû	(n.) cucumber
qitrubu	(n.) attack
rab šāqê	(n.) chief cupbearer
rākibu	(n.) rider
rēdû	(n.) soldier; administrator
rību (i)	(n.) earthquake
saḫpu	(aj.) covered
salāḫu	(v.; a-u) sprinkle (with)
sanqu	(aj.) disciplined
seḫpu	(n.) covering
ṣarāmu	(v.; i) make an effort
ṣêʾu	(v.; i) repulse
šādidu	(n.) one who drags
šaḫātu (i)	(n.) hiding place
šaḫurratu	(n.) deathly hush
šallaru	(n.) wall plaster
šamāṭu	(v.; a-u) tear away
šamūtu	(n.) rain

šassūru (n.) womb
šērtu (n.) punishment
šeṭû (v.; i) spread out
šību (n.) elder; witness
šikkû (n.) mongoose
šinnatu (n.) equality; similarity
šipṣu (n.) force
šumma (cnj.) if
šummuḫu (aj.) very luxuriant
šupālû (aj.) lower
šupālu (n.) depression; downwards
šuttinnu (n.) bat
takbittu (n.) honor
tāmarātu (n.) camels
tamḫu (aj.) holding
tīlāniš (av.) like tels (i.e., ruin mounds)
tiqnu (n.) ornament
ṭarpa'u (n.) (a variety of tamarisk)
urû (n.) team of equids; stable
waṣpu (n.) sling
wašru (aj.) humble; submissive
zâbu (v.; ū) dissolve
zakû (v.; u) be(come) exempt, clear
zārû (n.) progenitor
zi'pu (n.) mold
zû (n.) excrement

7 Occurrences

abāru **(ii)** (n.) physical strength
absinnu (n.) furrow
aḫulap (j.) (exclamation used to express compassion)
alālu (i) (n.) work song
ālilu (n.) brave one
amūtu (n.) liver
annanna (xp.) so-and-so; such-and-such
anuntu (n.) fight
aptu (n.) window
asakku (ii) (n.) taboo
ašamšūtu (n.) dust storm

banû (ii)	(v.; i) beautify
bāṣu	(n.) sand
bīnu	(n.) son; sprout
birītu (i)	(n.) alley; space between
birru	(n.) lattice
dāṣtu	(n.) disrespect
di'u (i)	(n.) (a disease affecting the head)
edēlu	(v.; i) shut
etelliš	(av.) akin to a lord
eṭûtu	(n.) darkness
ganūnu	(n.) private chamber
ginâ	(av.) constantly
giskimmu	(n.) sign
gupšu	(n.) surge
ḫābû	(n.) (a storage jar)
ḫalqu	(n.) runaway
ḫuliam	(n.) helmet
ḫupšu	(n.) (member of) lower class
ḫuribtu	(n.) desert
ibru	(n.) friend
illūriš	(av.) like a (red) flower
inû	(n.) craft
isḫappu	(n.) villain
kamāru (iv)	(v.; a-u) pile up
kīdu	(n.) outside
kitmusu	(aj.) folded; kneeling
kiūru	(n.) (a metal basin)
kudurru (ii)	(n.) boundary
lāma	(prp.) before (in time)
lasmu	(aj.) speedy
lawu	(aj.) surrounded
lē'u	(n.) board
maḫrâ	(aj.) older
māliktu	(n.) adviser
maltaktu	(n.) tested measure
mērešu (ii)	(n.) wisdom
mēzezu	(n.) wrath
mitru	(aj.) strong
muḫḫuriš	(av.) as an offering
mušaḫribu	(n.) one who devastates
mušakšidu	(n.) one who makes achieve

mūšaru	(n.) garden; area
mušēṣû	(n.) one who causes to go out
mušēšibu	(n.) one who settles
mūšiš	(av.) at night
mūterrišu	(n.) one who makes requests
nāḫiru	(n.) dolphin
nalbân	(av.) all around
nâlu	(v.; ā) strike down
nanmurtu	(n.) heliacal rising
napalsuḫu	(v.; N) fall to the ground
narmaku	(n.) washbowl
ne'rāru	(n.) aid; ally
nê'u	(v.; ē) turn back
neḫsu	(n.) inlay?
nepelkû	(v.; N) be(come) wide
nesû (ii)	(v.; e) drive away
nignakku	(n.) censer
nubattu	(n.) evening; vigil ceremonies
nupāru	(n.) (frame of) mind; heart
padānu	(n.) path
pāri'u	(n.) one who cuts through
paspasu	(n.) duck
pētû	(n.) one who opens
puquttu	(n.) thorn
qâdu	(v.; ū) ignite
qāmû	(n.) one who burns
qurunnu	(n.) heap; pile (of corpses)
ra'su	(n.) tribal chief
ramāku	(v.; u) bathe; wash
rapādu	(v.; u) roam
rapāsu	(v.; i) beat; pound
rēmūtu	(n.) mercy
riāšu	(v.; ī) rejoice
riḫiṣtu	(n.) destruction
rūqiš	(av.) from afar
ruqqû	(v.; D) make an aromatic
sammû	(n.) lyre
satālu	(v.; i) plant
simānu	(n.) season
sīrāšû	(n.) brewer
surqēnu	(n.) strewn offering

ṣarāḫu (i)	(v.; a-u) cry out
ṣēlu	(n.) side
šalpu	(aj.) unsheathed
šalputtu	(n.) ruination
šaqāru	(v.; i) pierce
šaqîš	(av.) high up
šarūru	(n.) brilliance
šatammu	(n.) (a chief administrator)
še'u	(n.) barley
šīḫu	(aj.) grown (tall)
šisītu	(n.) clamor; proclamation
šitnunu	(aj.) raised up to
šubultu	(n.) ear of corn
šukurru	(n.) lance; spear
taklīmu	(n.) (a food-offering)
taraḫḫu	(n.) fortified retaining wall
tuktû	(n.) revenge
ū'a	(j.) woe!
ūma	(av.) now; on this day
ūmiš	(av.) like a storm
ummān-manda	(n.) (a barbarous horde)
ūmu (ii)	(n.) storm; storm demon
urāsu	(n.) (a foreman)
ušparu	(n.) staff
utnēnu (ii)	(v.; ē) pray
wuššuru	(aj.) abandoned; freed
zaqpu	(aj.) erect(ed)
zīqīqiš	(av.) as nothing
zummu (ii)	(v.; D) deprive

6 Occurrences

a'lu	(n.) alliance (?)
abru (iii)	(n.) pile of brushwood
adīni	(av.) hitherto
amru	(aj.) agreeable; chosen; seen
apru	(aj.) with head covered
asakku (i)	(n.) (an evil demon)
ašāru	(v.; a-u) organize; review

aštammu	(n.) tavern woman
atappiš	(av.) like a canal
azaru	(n.) lynx
banû (iii)	(aj.) created
bâru (iii)	(v.; ū) be firm
bašāmu (iii)	(v.; a-u) allocate
baṭiltu	(n.) interruption
berâtu	(n.) waters
birtu (ii)	(n.) riffraff
bītānû	(aj.) inner
burḫiš	(n.) buffalo
diglu	(n.) (a mineral)
dilḫu	(n.) disturbance
erēḫu	(v.; i) attack
eṣēdu (i)	(n.) harvest
etelletu	(n.) pre-eminent one
eṭemmu	(n.) ghost
girim ḫilibê	(n.) (a precious stone)
girimmu	(n.) (a precious stone)
gištallu	(n.) crossbar
gištappu	(n.) footstool
ḫallālāniš	(av.) like a centipede
ḫāmimu	(n.) harvester
ḫāsisu	(n.) one who understands
ḫaṣānu	(v.; i) take under one's protection
ḫaṣāṣu	(v.; a-u) snap off
ḫātinu	(n.) protector
ḫatû	(v.; ?) (meaning unclear)
ḫāwiru	(n.) husband
ḫilibû	(n.) the underworld
ḫūšu	(n.) red (color)
ikku	(n.) mood
kakugallūtu	(n.) incantation priest
kaṣru	(aj.) firmly joined
kispu	(n.) (a funerary offering)
kulbābu	(n.) ant
kunnu	(aj.) established; fixed
kunzu	(n.) (a leather bag)
kurību	(n.) (an ethereal spirit)
kuṣṣuru	(aj.) thoroughly organized

labbūnu	(n.) (a stand or pedestal?)
labšu	(aj.) clothed
lāmidu	(n.) one who learns
laqātu	(v.; a-u) gather up
līṭūtu	(n.) role as hostage
magulû	(n.) (a big raft)
mākaltu	(n.) wooden dish
mamlu	(n.) impetuous one
masnaqtu	(n.) inspection
meḫṣu	(n.) (woven) textile
meṭlūtu	(n.) manhood
middatu	(n.) count(ing); dimension
mīs pî	(n.) (mouth-washing ritual)
mīsu	(n.) washing
miširtu	(n.) produce (of sea and rivers)
miṭṭu	(n.) (a divine weapon)
muḫalliqu	(n.) one who destroys
mušākilu	(n.) feeder
mušerbu	(n.) one who makes great
mutērtu	(n.) double door; leaf of a door
mutḫummu	(n.) fruit(s)
muttellu	(aj.) princely
muṭibbu (i)	(n.) one who makes pleasing
nadnu	(aj.) given
nagaltû	(v.; i) awake
naglabu	(n.) razor
napšu	(aj.) many?
naspantu	(n.) devastation
našarbuṭu	(v.; N) constantly chase about
nēpešu	(n.) activity; (siege) machine
nesûtu	(n.) distance
nidnu	(n.) gift
nukaribbu	(n.) gardener
nukkulu	(aj.) skillfully made
nulliātu	(n.) treachery
papparmīnu	(n.) (a white semiprecious stone)
parāṣu	(v.; a-u) lie; break an oath
pašqiš	(av.) with great effort
pazru	(aj.) hidden
pīt bābi	(n.) (an Elamite month)
pitluḫu	(aj.) feared

putuqqu	(aj.) constantly attentive
qītu	(n.) end
qurbūtu	(n.) bodyguard
rabābu	(v.; u) calm down; grow soft
rābiṣu	(n.) (a protective deity)
raksu (ii)	(n.) raft
ṣallamtu	(n.) basalt
ṣamādu (ii)	(v.; i) harness
ṣarpiš	(av.) loud and bitterly
ṣiātiš	(av.) for ever
ṣipru	(n.) (metal)spike
šabrû (ii)	(n.) interpreter of dreams
šalāmu (i)	(n.) (sun)set
šalṭāniš	(av.) in triumph
šamḫu	(aj.) prosperous
šarāṭu	(v.; a-u) tear
šēltu	(n.) sharp blade
šēlūtu	(n.) pointed blade
šinni ṣabīti	(n.) gazelle-tooth stone
šūlūtu	(n.) garrison?
šummannu	(n.) halter
šūnuḫu	(aj.) wearied, troubled
šutātû	(aj.) positioned opposite one another
šutbû	(aj.) raised
tāluku	(n.) course; march
tānēḫu	(n.) wailing
taṣliltu	(n.) roofing
tatīdu	(n.) (type of oak)
tēdištu	(n.) renewal
ti'ûtu	(n.) food
tikiltu	(n.) support
tīku	(n.) shower
tubqu	(n.) (outer) corner
turāḫu	(n.) ibex
uggugu	(aj.) angry
ulû	(n.) finest oil
urrākūtu	(n.) craft of the sculptor
utnēnu (i)	(n.) prayer
warāqu	(v.; i) be(come) pale
wasmu	(aj.) fitting; suitable
zamāru (i)	(n.) song

zarû	(v.; u) sow; scatter
zu''uzu	(aj.) divided
zūtu	(n.) sweat

5 Occurrences

abāku (ii)	(v.; a-u) overturn
abru (i)	(n.) humanity
abūsu	(n.) storehouse
agannutillû	(n.) dropsy
aḫā'iš	(rp.) one another
aḫḫūtu	(n.) brotherly relations
akanna	(av.) here
angubbû	(n.) (a class of priest)
anna	(j.) yes
asumittu	(n.) inscribed slab, stele
ašâtu	(n.) reins
atappu	(n.) (small) canal
atbaru	(n.) basalt
ayyaru (i)	(n.) rosette
ba'ālu	(v.; i) be very bright
battubattu	(prp.) all around
bēru (ii)	(aj.) choice; selected
dababtu	(n.) talk
dalāpu	(v.; i) (constantly) harass
dâlu	(v.; ū) move
damqiš	(av.) well
dapniš	(av.) violently
duppussû	(n.) younger brother
duššû	(aj.) abundant
edlu	(aj.) shut
egû	(v.; u) be negligent
ekēpu	(v.; i) come close; (D) be early
ekletu	(n.) darkness
ekmu	(aj.) taken away
elēlu (i)	(n.) cheerful song
enūtu	(n.) lordship
eriyātu	(n.) cold weather
esēpu	(v.; i) gather together
ettūtu	(n.) spider
gāmiru (i)	(aj.) strong

gamru	(aj.) complete
gišparru	(n.) trap
gunnu	(n.) main force? (of troops)
ḫalpu	(aj.) clad in
ḫammu (iii)	(aj.) gathered (to oneself)
ḫašālu	(v.; a-u) make crush
ḫelû	(v.; Š) illuminate; shine brightly
ḫesû	(v.; i) cover up; break up
ḫubūru	(n.) (a beer jar)
ḫullu	(n.) neck ring
ḫumṣīru	(n.) rat; large mouse
ḫuṣannu	(n.) belt
igigallu	(n.) wise man
ikû	(n.) (a measure); field
immu	(n.) daytime
inḫu	(n.) hardship
išittu	(n.) treasury
kabālu	(v.; a-u) be(come) paralyzed
kamsu	(aj.) kneeling
kappu (i)	(n.) wing
kawû (ii)	(n.) open country
kayyamānû	(aj.) reliable
kisalmāḫu	(n.) main court
kīsu	(n.) bag
kiṣir šadê	(n.) bedrock
kišubbāniš	(av.) into a waste
kizû	(n.) personal attendant
kuššudu	(aj.) chased (off)
la	(prp.) from
lâdiru	(aj.) fearless
lēʾûtu	(n.) competence; power
lezēnu	(v.; i) ridicule
līʾu	(n.) bull
maḫīriš	(av.) at market value
mākālu	(n.) food
makāṣu	(n.) slaughtering block
manziat	(n.) rainbow
mašāʾu	(v.; i) take away by force
meḫru (ii)	(n.) (a conifer)
mēlultu	(n.) game; sport
mesû (ii)	(v.; i) purify; wash

mētellu	(n.) power
mišītu	(n.) oblivion
mitḫartu	(n.) (side of a) square; mankind
mugallitu	(n.) intimidator
mullilu	(n.) cleanser
munakkipu	(n.) one who gores
munnarbu	(n.) fugitive; swift
mupaḫḫiru	(n.) one who gathers
mupaššiṭu	(n.) one who erases
mupparkû	(n.) that which ceases
mupparšu	(aj.) flying; winged
murtê'u	(n.) one who shepherds
mušāpû	(n.) one who makes manifest
mušḫarmiṭu	(n.) one who dissolves
muttalliku	(aj.) mobile; able to march
muttinnu	(n.) choice wine
muzzapru	(aj.) very bad
nagāru	(n.) carpenter
nakāmu	(v.; a-u/i) amass
nalbattu	(n.) brick mold; frame
namriš	(av.) splendidly
narbû	(n.) greatness
nāriš	(av.) like a river
nawû (ii)	(v.; D) be a desert
nēmattu	(n.) couch
nigiṣṣu	(n.) crevice
nišku	(n.) bite
nu''udu	(aj.) very praiseworthy
nuballu	(n.) eagle's wing; vanguard
nukurtu	(n.) enmity; hostility
palāšu	(v.; a-u) pierce
palḫu	(aj.) frightened; reverent
paršu	(n.) excrement
pašīšu	(n.) (a priest)
pattūtu	(n.) open chariot
pīqu	(aj.) narrow
pīt pî	(n.) (a ritual)
pittu	(n.) accordingly; adjacent region
pūru (ii)	(n.) lot
qā'išu	(n.) giver
qebēru	(v.; i) bury

qudmu	(n.) front; ancient times
qulliu	(n.) (a vessel)
qulmû	(n.) (kind of) axe
qutrēnu	(n.) incense (offering)
rādu	(n.) downpour
rakbu	(aj.) riding
ramku	(n.) (a cultic functionary)
rēšūtu	(n.) slavery
rimku	(n.) (a washing ceremony)
ritpāšu	(aj.) vast
salātu (i)	(n.) family
samānēšret	(nu.) eighteen
sangilimud	(n.) (a blue stone)
sukku	(n.) shrine
summatu	(n.) female dove
surriš	(av.) quickly
ṣēriš	(av.) towards; upon
ṣibtu (ii)	(n.) interest
ṣiddu	(n.) proletariat
ṣummû	(n.) thirst
šāpirūtu	(n.) sovereignty
šarrāqiš	(av.) like a thief
šarû	(v.; u) be(come) rich
šâšina	(ip.) those
šēlabiš	(av.) like a fox
šiāṭu	(v.; ī) be(come) neglectful
šina	(ip.) they
šitpuru	(aj.) armed; shrouded
šuātina	(ip.) those
šuḫrubu	(aj.) devastated; uncultivated
šuḫṭu	(n.) anger
šumru	(n.) fury
šuparzuḫu	(v.; Š) make abundant
taḫūmu	(n.) border; boundary stone
tamītu	(n.) oath
tapšuḫtu	(n.) rest
tēliltu	(n.) (ritual) cleansing
tēšû	(n.) melee
tiṣbutu	(aj.) connected to; grasping
turminû	(n.) (a breccia or marble)
tūrtu	(n.) return

ulla (i) (j.) no!
urītu (n.) mare
wardatu (n.) young woman
waršu (aj.) dirty
wāṣītu (n.) that which goes out
watmu (n.) hatchling
wiāṣu (v.; ī) be(come) too little, small
yašpû (n.) jasper
zāʾerūtu (n.) enmity
zêru (v.; ē) dislike
zīqīqu (n.) phantom

Notes

APPENDIX A: PRONOMINAL SUFFIXES

This appendix includes both verbal and nominal pronominal suffixes. Because these suffixes are inseparable, they do not appear in the frequency lists. However, due to their significant semantic content, you should be aware of them. This is particularly necessary because the Standard Babylonian of Assyrian royal inscriptions tends to prefer Assyrian-style pronominal suffixes for verbs rather than the Old Babylonian forms to which most students are first exposed.

Verbal Pronominal Suffixes (Accusative)

Person	Accusative Singular	Babylonian Accusative Plural	Assyrian Accusative Plural
1st c	-anni (else) -nni (2nd f sg) -ninni (pl vocalic)	-niāti	-nāši
2nd m	-ka	-kunūti	-kunu
2nd f	-ki	-kināti	-kina
3rd m	-šu	-šunūti	-šunu
3rd f	-ši	-šināti	-šina

Verbal Pronominal Suffixes (Dative)

Person	Dative Singular	Babylonian Dative Plural	Assyrian Dative Plural[a]
1st c	-am (else) -m (2nd f sg) -nim (pl vocalic)	-niāšim	-nāši
2nd m	-ku(m)	-kunūšim	-kunūti
2nd f	-ki(m)	-kināšim	-kināti
3rd m	-šu(m)	-šunūšim	-šunūti
3rd f	-ši(m)	-šināšim	-šināti

[a]Note that the Standard Babylonian of the Neo-Assyrian era tends to collapse the distinction between dative and accusative verbal pronominal suffixes in favor of accusative forms.

Nominal/Prepositional Pronominal Suffixes (Genitive)

Person	Singular	Plural
1st c	-ya (else) -ī (nom/acc sg)	-ni
2nd m	-ka	-kunu
2nd f	-ki	-kina
3rd m	-šu	-šunu
3rd f	-ša	-šina

APPENDIX B: STANDARD BABYLONIAN PHONOLOGY

As stated in the introduction, the words contained in this book are given in their Old Babylonian form (minus mimation).[1] However, Assyrian royal inscriptions are written in a variety of dialects, including Middle Assyrian and Standard Babylonian. Because the majority of Assyrian royal inscriptions—including the Sargonid inscriptions—are written in Standard Babylonian, this means that the forms of words you will encounter while reading Assyrian royal inscriptions are not necessarily identical to those contained in this book. A similar situation obtains for the *CDA*, which also uses Old Babylonian word forms despite covering all periods of Akkadian. Students should, then, gain facility in moving between Old and Standard Babylonian forms of words as part of their use of the language.

What follows is intended to aid you in that endeavor by drawing attention to some of the major phonological changes that distinguish Old and Standard Babylonian from each other. For further information, you should consult Huehnergard 2011, 595–98, and Hess 2020.

Changes Involving /w/

The /w/ sound undergoes two major changes in Standard Babylonian.

The first is the loss of word-initial *w*-. This means that words beginning with *wa*- in Old Babylonian instead begin with *a*- in Standard Babylonian. For example, the common verbs *wabālu* ("to bring, carry") and *wašābu* ("to sit, dwell") appear instead as *abālu* and *ašābu* in Standard Babylonian, and the common noun *wardu* ("slave") appears as *ardu*.

1. Mimation—the presence of a final *m* after a case ending on nouns, adjectives, and infinitives—was already disappearing by the late Old Babylonian period.

TIP: When you encounter a word that begins with *a*- that you don't recognize, ask yourself if you know it as a *wa*- word.

The second /w/ change is the transformation of intervocalic /w/ (i.e., *w* appearing between two vowels) into an /m/ sound. This means that words containing a *w* between two vowels in Old Babylonian will instead be spelled with an *m* in that position in Standard Babylonian. For example, words such as *awīlu* ("man") and *awātu* ("word") appear instead as *amīlu* and *amātu*. Note that this can occur in verbal forms where the *w* may have been lost from the infinitive itself, so that, for example, *ašāru* ("to sink down") becomes *umaššar* in the D-stem durative.

TIP: When you encounter a word that you don't recognize spelled with an *m* between two vowels, ask yourself if you know it as a word with a *w* in that position instead.

š to *l* Before Dentals

In Standard Babylonian, the sound /š/ becomes an /l/ when it is immediately followed by a dental sound (/d/, /t/, /ṭ/).

One commonly encountered case of this transformation can be seen in the preposition *ištu* ("from"), which appears as *ultu* in Standard Babylonian texts.

This change is also commonly seen in words that have a final *š* followed by a feminine ending, such as Old Babylonian *lubuštu* ("clothing"), which is spelled *lubultu* in Standard Babylonian. Note that this change can occur in tandem with other expected changes, such as in the feminine verbal adjective of *marāṣu* ("to be sick"). Where the final *ṣ* becomes *š* before the feminine ending in Old Babylonian, Standard Babylonian then transforms this to an *l*. This leads Old Babylonian *maruštu* to sometimes appear as Standard Babylonian *marultu*.

Another common case of this transformation is in verbs where the first root letter is *š* and the second root is a dental, such as *šaṭāru* ("to write"). Where Old Babylonian would render its preterite as *ašṭur*, Standard Babylonian is more likely to render it as *alṭur*. Several verbal forms, such as the Gt/n and Dt/n will also bring a verb starting with *š* into a position where the *š* is rendered as *l*. Finally, Št/n verbs frequently undergo this change as well, with the characteristic *š* prefix appearing as an *l*.

Note that this phonological change is not consistently represented in Standard Babylonian texts—you will still encounter numerous cases where a /š/ plus dental combination is still written with *š*.

TIP: When you encounter a word spelled with a *ld*, *lt*, or *lṭ* that you don't recognize, ask yourself if you know it as a *šd*, *št*, or *šṭ* word instead.

-t- Infix Vocalization

In Standard Babylonian, the /t/ sound that occurs as an infix in the perfect tense and in various derived verbal stems assimilates its voicing to preceding consonants. This means that the /t/ sound instead becomes a /d/ sound when it is preceded by a voiced consonant such as *b*, *d*, *g*, and *m*.

Take the common verb *gamāru* ("to complete, destroy"), for example. Whereas Old Babylonian would render its perfect as *agtamar*, Standard Babylonian is more likely to render it as *agdamar*. Another example is the D perfect of *malû* ("to be full"). Where Old Babylonian would render it as *umtalli*, Standard Babylonian is more likely to write *umdalli*. Note that sometimes the combination *mt* is instead rendered *nd*, such as in the perfect D stem of *wašāru* ("to sink down"; D "to release"), which is rendered *undaššar* instead of *umdaššar*.

TIP: When you encounter a verbal form that has a *d* immediately following a voiced consonant, ask yourself if it is more recognizable with a *t* in place of the *d*.

Vowel Contraction

In general, Standard Babylonian displays a greater level of vowel contraction than Old Babylonian. This is most notable in nouns and adjectives that end in -*i*. Take *rabû* ("great"), for example; whereas Old Babylonian would write its accusative form as *rabiam*, Standard Babylonian would render it *rabâ*, with full contraction.

Prevalence of *e* Vowels

Due to the influence of Assyrian, Standard Babylonian may sometimes have an *e* vowel where Old Babylonian would have an *a* or *i* vowel.

One common case is in the word *awīlu* ("man, person"), which is rendered in Standard Babylonian as either *amīlu* or *amēlu*.

Precatives in *lu-/la-*

Due to the influence of Assyrian, Standard Babylonian may sometimes adopt Assyrian vocalization for the precative forms of verbs. Whereas Old Babylonian has distinctive precative prefixes, such as *li-* for the 3rd masculine singular and *lu-* for the 1st common singular, Standard Babylonian may follow the Assyrian practice of merely prefixing an *l-* to the preterite form of the verb to produce the precative. Whereas Old Babylonian would have the D stem precative *lipaḫḫir* ("may he gather"), Standard Babylonian may have either this form or the Assyrianizing *lupaḫḫir*.

TIP: Make sure to pay attention to context to help you disambiguate persons of the precative.

3rd Feminine Singular Finite Verbs

While not a phonological issue, one common morphological feature deserves brief comment. Due to the influence of Assyrian, Standard Babylonian may use a distinctive 3rd feminine singular verbal form rather than the Old Babylonian 3rd common singular. This form uses the prefix *ta-* and will, then, look identical to the 2nd masculine singular form. For example, in Old Babylonian, the form *tašbir* would have to be understood as "you broke." However, in Standard Babylonian, this may also mean "she broke."

TIP: Make sure to pay attention to context to help you disambiguate the meaning of *ta-* prefixes.

APPENDIX C: VERB VOWEL CLASSES

This appendix lists the vowel class of all verbs appearing in Chapters 1–10. (Note also that verb classes appear with the verbs in the lists themselves.) The numbers appearing in parentheses after each verb identifies which list in this book contains that verb. As is standard practice, when two vowels are listed, the first indicates the vowel of the G durative and perfect, while the second indicates the vowel of the G preterite.

For II-weak verbs, we have indicated the appropriate vowel class, conditioned by the lost consonant, with a macron (ā, ī, ū, ē). For III-weak verbs, you should be aware that the vowel indicated is the remnant of the lost final consonant.

In some cases, we have used a capital D or Š to indicate that you will primarily encounter a verb in the indicated derived stem. In those instances, stem verbs are vowel class a-i. In other cases, we have used a capital N to indicate that you will primarily encounter a verb in the N stem. While the majority of N stem verbs are vowel class a-i, some are strictly i-class. Students should consult *CAD* if context cannot help them distinguish the durative form from the preterite form of these verbs. The absence of one of these symbols does not necessarily indicate that the G stem occurs in the Assyrian royal inscription corpus.

Note that some of the vowel classes in this appendix may differ from those you learn from the major grammars of Akkadian, which tend to focus primarily on Old Babylonian. This is due to shifts in vowel class in Standard Babylonian, as well as basic differences between the Assyrian and Babylonian dialects that occasionally influenced how Assyrian scribes spelled words in Assyrian royal inscriptions. Students should also be aware that Assyrian vowel shading will sometimes render expected "i" class verbs as "e" class.

abāku (i) (10.14)	a-u
abāku (ii) (10.5)	a-u
abātu (i) (4-B)	a-u
abātu (ii) (2-D)	a-u
adāru (4-E)	a-u
agāgu (8-H)	a-u
aḫāzu (5-C)	a-u
akālu (5-G)	a-u
alāku (1-B)	a-i
alālu (ii) (6-C)	a-u
amāru (2-B)	a-u
anāḫu (2-C)	a
apālu (5-G)	a-u
apāru (7-H)	i
arāḫu (9-A)	a
arāku (4-E)	i
arāru (7-C)	a-u
ašāru (10.6)	a-u
awû (9-F)	u
baʾālu (10.5)	i
bâʾu (6-E)	ā
babālu (10.9)	a-i
balālu (8-F)	a-u
balāṭu (ii) (5-A)	a
banû (ii) (10.7)	i
banû (iv) (3-B)	i
baqāmu (10.11)	a-u
barāqu (10.14)	i
barû (i) (6-C)	i
bâru (iii) (10.6)	ū
bâru (i) (9-A)	ā
bašāmu (iii) (10.6)	a-u
bašāmu (ii) (10.14)	i
bašû (i) (3-A)	i
batāqu (5-B)	a-u
baṭālu (7-C)	i
bêlu (3-A)	ē
biātu (4-E)	ī
bitrû (ii) (8-H)	i
buʾʾû (10.11)	D
dabābu (ii) (6-E)	u
dagālu (4-C)	a-u
dâku (2-B)	ū
dalālu (7-G)	a-u
dalāpu (10.5)	i
dâlu (10.5)	ū
danānu (ii) (4-A)	i
daqāqu (9-D)	D
dekû (2-D)	e
diānu (10.13)	ī
diāšu (10.10)	ī
ebēbu (10.8)	i
ebēru (2-E)	i
edēlu (10.7)	i
edēšu (2-C)	i
edû (ii) (5-E)	e
egû (10.5)	u
ekēmu (3-C)	i
ekēpu (10.5)	i
elēlu (ii) (8-F)	i
elēṣu (6-F)	i
elû (iii) (2-C)	i
emēdu (2-D)	i
enēšu (8-F)	i
enû (6-C)	i
epēšu (1-B)	u
erēbu (2-A)	u
erēḫu (10.6)	i
erēšu (ii) (7-H)	i
esēpu (10.5)	i
esēqu (10.11)	i
esēru (ii) (5-C)	i
eṣēdu (ii) (10.10)	i
eṣēru (9-F)	i
ešēru (3-A)	i
etēqu (4-A)	i
eṭēru (6-F)	i
ewû (5-B)	e
ezēbu (2-C)	i
ezēzu (9-B)	i
galātu (10.8)	u
gamālu (10.8)	i

gamāru (6-F)	a-u	kânu (2-A)	ū
gapāšu (10.8)	u	kapādu (5-D)	u/i
gerû (9-F)	i	karābu (5-F)	a-u
ḫabābu (7-I)	u	karû (ii) (9-H)	i
ḫabālu (9-H)	i	kasāru (8-C)	i
ḫabātu (i) (5-F)	a-u	kasû (iii) (8-B)	i
ḫabû (10.10)	u	kaṣāru (4-A)	i
ḫadû (iii) (10.9)	u	kâṣu (8-F)	ū
ḫalāpu (7-G)	u	kašādu (1-B)	a-u
ḫalāqu (3-A)	i	kašāru (7-F)	i
ḫâlu (10.10)	ī	kašāṭu (7-C)	i
ḫamāṭu (iii) (10.8)	a-u	katāmu (5-F)	a-u
ḫamāṭu (ii) (10.9)	u	katāru (8-B)	i
ḫanābu (10.11)	u	kullu (iii) (9-H)	D
ḫarābu (6-C)	u	kullumu (4-D)	D
ḫarāṣu (10.8)	a-u	labānu (5-C)	i
ḫasāsu (6-F)	a-u	labāru (3-E)	i
ḫaṣānu (10.6)	i	labāšu (5-D)	i
ḫaṣāṣu (10.6)	a-u	lamādu (9-B)	a
ḫašāḫu (6-C)	a-u	lapātu (7-H)	a-u
ḫašālu (10.5)	a-u	laqātu (10.6)	a-u
ḫatānu (10.8)	i	lâṭu (10.8)	ū
ḫatû (10.6)	(?)	lawû (ii) (2-D)	i
ḫaṭû (5-D)	i	lemēnu (10.13)	i
ḫelû (10.5)	Š	leqû (3-C)	e
ḫepû (ii) (10.13)	i	lezēnu (10.5)	i
ḫerû (5-F)	i	mâdu (9-D)	ī
ḫesû (10.5)	i	magāru (5-G)	a-u
ḫiāšu (10.9)	ī	maḫāru (2-A)	a-u
ḫiāṭu (10.13)	ī	maḫāṣu (2-E)	a
išû (i) (3-A)	i/u	makāru (7-H)	i
itūlu (10.11)	ī	malāku (8-H)	i
izuzzu (2-B)	a-i	malû (iv) (3-A)	a
kabālu (10.5)	a-u	manû (iv) (2-B)	u
kabāru (i) (7-H)	i	maqātu (2-D)	u
kabāsu (5-A)	a-u	marāru (7-I)	i
kalû (v) (5-B)	a	masāku (8-C)	Š
kamāru (iv) (10.7)	a-u	maṣû (6-F)	i
kamāsu (ii) (9-A)	i	mašā'u (10.5)	i
kamû (ii) (10.8)	i	mašāḫu (10.13)	a-u
kanāšu (2-B)	u	mašû (ii) (5-G)	i

mesû (ii) (10.5)	i	natāru (10.13)	Š
mêšu (8-E)	ē	naṭālu (7-B)	a-u
naʾādu (10.12)	i	nawāru (4-A)	i
nabalkutu (ii) (3-B)	N	nawû (ii) (10.5)	D
nabāṭu (10.10)	u	nêʾu (10.7)	ē
nabû (ii) (3-A)	i	nekelmû (7-I)	N
nadānu (ii) (3-A)	i	nepelkû (10.7)	N
nadāru (10.13)	N	neqelpû (10.8)	N
nâdu (i) (9-B)	ā	nêru (i) (4-A)	ē
nadû (iii) (2-B)	i	nesû (ii) (10.7)	e
nagaltû (10.6)	i	paḫāru (ii) (4-D)	u
nagāšu (10.14)	u	palāḫu (3-B)	a
naḫarmuṭu (10.14)	Š	palāku (10.8)	a-u
nâḫu (6-D)	ū	palāqu (10.9)	i
nakādu (10.8)	u	palāsu (4-B)	a-u
nakālu (7-F)	i	palāšu (10.5)	a-u
nakāmu (10.5)	a-u/i	paqādu (5-A)	i
nakāpu (i) (10.8)	i	parāʾu (8-G)	a-u
nakāru (3-A)	i	parāku (9-E)	i
nakāsu (3-A)	i	parāru (6-C)	u
nâlu (10.7)	ā	parāsu (5-A)	a-u
namāšu (2-D)	u	parāṣu (10.6)	a-u
napāḫu (9-A)	a-u	pašāḫu (6-A)	a
napalsuḫu (10.7)	N	pašālu (9-A)	i
napālu (2-B)	a-u	pašāqu (8-D)	u
napardû (ii) (10.8)	N	pašāru (10.10)	a-u
naparkû (ii) (7-D)	N	pašāšu (4-A)	a-u
naparšudu (3-E)	N	pašāṭu (4-E)	i
napāṣu (10.14)	a-u	patāqu (6-A)	i
napāšu (9-G)	u	paṭāru (6-B)	a-u
naprušu (6-A)	N	petû (ii) (3-D)	e
naqāru (2-B)	a-u	puqqu (10.13)	D
naqû (2-E)	i	qabû (2-B)	i
narāṭu (10.11)	u	qâdu (10.7)	ū
nasāḫu (3-C)	a-u	qalû (ii) (10.14)	i
nasāku (8-A)	u	qamû (3-D)	i/u
nasāqu (8-E)	a-u/i	qanānu (10.9)	a-u
naṣāru (4-B)	a-u	qâpu (9-I)	ū
našāqu (3-D)	i	qarānu (9-E)	a-u
našarbuṭu (10.6)	N	qatû (ii) (5-E)	i
našû (ii) (2-E)	i	qebēru (10.5)	i

qerēbu (2-E)	i	seḫû (10.13)	i
qerû (7-G)	i	sekēru (10.9)	i
qiāšu (4-A)	ī	siāqu (9-G)	ī
qu''û (10.9)	D	suppû (8-D)	D
rabābu (10.6)	u	ṣabātu (1-C)	a
rabāṣu (9-A)	i	ṣalā'u (7-B)	i
rabû (ii) (3-C)	i	ṣalālu (9-G)	a
râbu (9-C)	ū	ṣamādu (ii) (10.6)	i
radādu (10.11)	a-u	ṣamāru (10.9)	D
raḫāṣu (i) (10.10)	i	ṣarāḫu (i) (10.7)	a-u
raḫāṣu (ii) (8-B)	i/u	ṣarāḫu (iii) (9-C)	a-u
rakābu (6-B)	a	ṣarāmu (10.8)	i
rakāsu (3-D)	a-u	ṣarāpu (6-B)	a-u
ramāku (10.7)	u	ṣarāšu (10.13)	D
ramû (iii) (10.9)	u	ṣê'u (10.8)	i
ramû (ii) (3-E)	i	ṣeḫēru (7-A)	i
râmu (ii) (5-E)	ā	ṣubbû (10.13)	D
rapādu (10.7)	u	ṣullû (4-E)	D
rapāsu (10.7)	i	ṣullulu (ii) (10.10)	D
rapāšu (5-A)	i	šâ'u (10.9)	ū
rasābu (5-A)	i	šabāsu (9-I)	u
raṣāpu (3-B)	i	šadādu (5-E)	a-u
rašādu (5-G)	Š	šadāḫu (8-G)	i
rašû (3-D)	i	šadālu (6-C)	i
re'û (7-E)	e	šagāmu (7-I)	u
redû (i) (2-B)	e	šagāšu (10.13)	i
retû (ii) (4-E)	i	šaḫātu (iii) (8-D)	u
riābu (10.13)	ī	šaḫāṭu (i) (10.11)	i
riāšu (10.7)	ī	šaḫāṭu (ii) (7-E)	a-u
ruqqû (10.7)	D	šakānu (1-B)	a-u
sadāru (9-C)	i	šalālu (1-C)	a-u
saḫālu (10.12)	a-u	šalāmu (ii) (3-E)	i
saḫāpu (3-A)	a-u	šalāpu (10.9)	a-u
saḫāru (5-B)	u	šalû (ii) (9-E)	u
sakāpu (4-C)	i	šâlu (4-E)	ā
salāḫu (10.8)	a-u	šamāḫu (7-E)	u
salātu (ii) (10.12)	a	šamāru (i) (10.14)	u
sanāqu (9-C)	i	šamāṭu (10.8)	a-u
sapāḫu (6-D)	a-u	šâmu (10.14)	ā
sapānu (4-D)	a-u	šanānu (4-B)	a-u
satālu (10.7)	i	šanû (iv) (5-D)	i

šanû (iii) (5-G)	i
šapāku (6-B)	a-u
šapālu (8-B)	i
šapāru (2-C)	a-u
šaqāru (10.7)	i
šaqû (ii) (6-B)	u
šaqû (iii) (9-C)	i
šarāḫu (4-D)	D
šarāku (3-E)	a-u
šarāpu (3-A)	a-u
šarāṭu (10.6)	a-u
šarû (10.5)	u
šasû (5-G)	i
šatû (ii) (8-E)	i
šaṭāru (2-E)	a-u
šâṭu (i) (6-A)	ū
šeʾû (5-C)	i
šebēru (6-F)	
šebû (6-B)	i
šêlu (8-E)	D
šemû (2-A)	e
šêtu (10.12)	ē/ī
šeṭû (10.8)	i
šiāḫu (9-C)	ī
šiāmu (5-A)	ī
šiāṭu (10.5)	ī
šuklulu (ii) (2-D)	Š
šuparzuḫu (10.5)	Š
šutlumu (4-D)	Š
tabāku (5-A)	a-u
tabālu (7-I)	a
takālu (2-E)	a/i
tamāḫu (4-D)	a-u
tamû (10.9)	a
taqānu (8-H)	u
tarāku (7-C)	a-u
tarāṣu (4-B)	a-u
târu (1-C)	ū
tebû (4-B)	i
ṭabāḫu (8-G)	a-u
ṭarādu (9-C)	a-u
ṭebû (9-A)	u
ṭeḫû (8-B)	e
ṭiābu (5-B)	ī
utnēnu (ii) (10.7)	ē
wabālu (2-A)	a-i
wadû (10.13)	D
walādu (7-D)	a-i
wapû (8-A)	i
waqāru (8-A)	i
waqû (10.10)	i
warādu (3-E)	a-i
warāqu (10.6)	i
warû (4-C)	u
wâru (3-C)	ā
wasāmu (5-E)	D
waṣābu (10.11)	a-i
waṣû (2-B)	i
wašābu (2-A)	a-i
wašāru (2-E)	D
watāru (4-C)	i
watû (7-D)	a
wiāṣu (10.5)	ī
wussû (6-F)	D
wuṣṣû (10.9)	D
zaʾānu (7-F)	D
zabālu (9-E)	i
zâbu (10.8)	ū
zakāru (3-E)	a-u
zakû (10.8)	u
zanānu (ii) (10.12)	a-u
zanānu (i) (7-I)	u
zaqāpu (4-C)	a-u
zaqāru (6-D)	D
zarû (10.6)	u
zâzu (6-B)	ū
zêru (10.5)	ē
ziāqu (10.13)	ī
zummu (ii) (10.7)	D

APPENDIX D: LOGOGRAM LIST I (SUMERIAN-AKKADIAN)

In this appendix, you will find a near-exhaustive list of the logograms appearing in the corpus of Assyrian royal inscriptions (excluding proper nouns), along with their Akkadian readings. Each Akkadian word will be followed by the list in which it appears in chapters 1–10 of this book. When no list is provided, this indicates that the word occurs fewer than five times in the Assyrian royal inscription corpus. Students should consult the *CDA* or one of the other standard dictionaries in these cases.

In building this appendix, we have followed the policy of RIAo in treating determinatives as the first part of the spelling of a logogram (i.e., without distinguishing them from other parts of logographic writing by superscripting). The one exception to this has been the divine determinative, which is represented by a superscript "d" and is not considered part of the spelling for alphabetizing purposes. For a list of determinatives and their meanings, you should consult Miller and Shipp 2014, 254–59. Among the most common determinatives that may or may not occur in a particular logographic writing is the sign LÚ. If you encounter a logogram and do not find it in the index, add a LÚ to the beginning and check for that entry.

In designing this appendix, we have had to confront the fact that the RIAo project contains texts that were edited as parts of different projects, by different hands, in different decades. This has caused a degree of inconsistency in the renderings of certain logograms, such as the readings GIŠ.KU.AN and GIŠ.TUKUL.DINGIR for the Akkadian miṭṭu ("divine weapon"). These readings represent the same underlying cuneiform, and, in instances such as this, we have chosen to include both readings in this index to help you locate the proper Akkadian. In other words, this index has been designed to help you read texts as published in RIAo, RIMA, and RINAP, rather than presenting a scientifically rigorous and consistent view of the logographic writings system(s) at use in Assyrian royal inscriptions.

Notes About Logographic Writings

Students should be aware that nouns derived from other substantives (such as abstracts and adverbs) are often spelled with the logogram of the substantive plus phonetic complements (e.g., EN-ti for bēlūti or SIG_5-iš for damqiš). We have not included separate entries for these types of logographic usage. In any give instance, you should consider whether a different derivative better fits the syntactic role that the logogram plays in a sentence, whether a phonetic complement is present or not. For example, while GIBIL will only point to eššu in this appendix, this logogram can also be read as eššūtu or eššiš, even when phonetic complements are lacking.

Students should also be aware that logographic writing can be used to convey grammatical information about the underlying Akkadian form, such as SIG_5 for masculine damqu and MUNUS.SIG_5 for feminine damiqtu. In some cases, either logographic writing or phonetic complementation may play this role. For example, the logogram KAL (dannu) can express the feminine dannatu (with specialized meanings) as either KAL-te or MUNUS.KAL. Students should be aware of the complex interactions between logographic and syllabic writing when considering how best to understand and translate a word they encounter.

Students should also be aware of other information encoded into logographic writing. For example, both GIŠ.MAR.GÍD.DA and MUL.MAR.GÍD.DA (both contained in this index) denote the Akkadian reading ereqqu. However, the GIŠ ("wood") determinative in the first instance indicates that a literal wagon is in view, while the MUL ("star") determinative of the second indicates that the referent is a constellation.

All of this is to say that you should not only look at the logogram and its Akkadian reading in this index but also consider the phonetic complements, determinatives, and context.

2	šanûti- (9-A)
2.30	šumēla (7-E)
2.30	šumēlu (10.13)
3	šalāšī- (9-I)
3	šalšu (8-A)
4	rebû (8-A)
6	šeššu (i) (10.14)
7	sebîšu
7	sebû (10.10)
8	samānû (10.14)
9	tišû
11	ištēnšerû

12	šinšariu
13	šalaššerû
^{d}15	ištaru (4-C)
18	samānēšret (10.5)
60	šūši (4-E)
A	māru (1-A)
A	mû (2-D)
A.AB.BA	tiāmtu (1-C)
A.BÁR	abāru (ii) (10.7)
A.GÀR	ugāru (7-B)
A.KAL	mīlu (4-C)
A.MU.RU	šarāku (3-E)
A.RÁ	arû
A.ŠÀ	eqlu (4-D)
A.ZU	ṭupšarru (7-H)
Á	emūqu (3-B)
Á	idu (3-A)
Á	ittu (i) (8-B)
Á.GÁL	lēʾû (5-D)
Á.KAL	emūqu (3-B)
Á.TAḪ	rēṣūtu (4-B)
AB	tiāmtu (1-C)
AB.SAR	šaṭru (3-C)
AB.SÍN	absinnu (10.7)
AB.ZU	apsû (6-C)
ÁB.GU$_4$	lītu (ii)
ABGAL	apkallu (6-D)
AD	abu (1-C)
AD.ḪAL	pirištu (7-E)
AD.ME.KÁR	šattu (3-B)
ADDA	pagru (4-B)
ADDA	šalamtu (6-E)
ÁG	râmu (ii) (5-E)
AGA	agû (i) (5-C)
ÁGA	narāmu (4-B)
ÁGA	rāʾimu (5-B)
ÁGA	râmu (ii) (5-E)
AGARIN$_4$	rēmu (4-E)
AL.TIL	gamru (10.5)
^{d}ALAD	šēdu (7-D)
^{d}ALAD.LAMMA	aladlammû (5-E)

ALAM	ṣalmu (ii) (2-C)
ALAM.DÍM	alandimmû
AM	rīmu (5-C)
AM.SI	pīru (3-D)
AMA	ummu (i) (5-E)
AMAR	būru (ii) (10.9)
AN	šamû (2-B)
AN.BAR	parzillu (3-B)
AN.DÙL	andullu (8-F)
AN.DÙL	ṣulūlu (6-C)
AN.GUB.BA	angubbû (10.5)
AN.MI	antallû
AN.NA	annaku (4-D)
AN.PA	elât šamê
AN.TA	elēnû (7-E)
AN.TA	eliš (5-E)
AN.TA	elītu (10.8)
AN.TA	elû (ii)
AN.TA	elû (i) (5-A)
AN.ÚR	išid šamê
ANŠE	imēru (i) (3-C)
ANŠE	imēru (ii) (5-F)
ANŠE.A.AB.BA	gammalu (4-B)
ANŠE.A.AB.BA	ibilu (6-D)
ANŠE.EDIN.NA	serrēmu (10.13)
ANŠE.GAM.MAL	gammalu (4-B)
ANŠE.GÌR.NUN.NA	kūdanu (5-G)
ANŠE.KUNGA	parû (i) (3-D)
ANŠE.KUR	sisû (2-A)
ANŠE.KUR.RA	sisû (2-A)
ANŠE.NÍTA	imēru (i) (3-C)
ANŠE.NUN	damdāmu
ARḪUŠ	rēmu (4-E)
AS$_4$.LUM	aslu (ii) (5-G)
AŠ.A.AN	kawû (i)
AŠ.ÀM	ištēn (3-E)
AZ	asu (10.10)
AZAG	asakku (ii) (10.7)
ÁZAG	asakku (i) (10.6)
BA	qiāšu (4-A)
BÀ	amūtu (10.7)

BABBAR	peṣû (4-E)
BAD	petû (i) (7-A)
BÀD	dūru (i) (2-B)
BÀD.KI	dūru (i) (2-B)
BÀD.ŠUL.ḪI	šalḫû (6-B)
BÀD.ŠUL.ḪU	šalḫû (6-B)
BAD_4	dannatu (4-C)
$BAD_5.BAD_5$	dabdû (2-E)
BAL	enû (6-C)
BAL	nabalkutu (ii) (3-B)
BAL	nabalkutu (i)
BAL	naqû (2-E)
$BAL.GI.KU_6$	raqqu (ii)
BALA	palû (2-A)
BÁN	sūtu
BAR	kidinnu (8-E)
BÁRA	parakku (3-C)
BÁRA.MAḪ	paramāḫu (9-I)
BI	šī (5-E)
BI.LUL	šāqû
BIR	sapḫu (10.11)
BU.BU.LU	šiteʾû
BULUG	pulukku (10.8)
BUR	pūru (i)
BUR.GUL	parkullu
BUR.SAG.GÁ	bursaggû
BÚR	pašāru (10.10)
BÚR.GAL	ušumgallu (8-A)
$BURU_5$	erbû (8-H)
$BURU_{14}$	ebūru (6-A)
DAB	ṣabātu (1-C)
DAGAL	rapšu (2-C)
DAGAL	rupšu (6-E)
DAM	aššatu (5-C)
DANNA	bēru (iii) (4-C)
DAR.LUGAL.MUŠEN	tarlugallu (10.9)
DÀRA	turāḫu (10.6)
DÀRA.MAŠ	ayyalu (10.10)
$DI.KU_5$	dayyānu (6-C)
$DI.KU_5.GAL$	dikuggallu (10.12)
DI.KUD	uršānu (7-I)

DI.KUD.GAL	dikuggallu (10.12)
DIB	etēqu (4-A)
DIB	ṣabātu (1-C)
DIDA	billatu
DINGIR	ilu (1-A)
DIŠ	šumma (10.8)
DU	alāku (1-B)
DU	āliku (2-C)
DÙ	bānû (2-D)
DÙ	epēšu (1-B)
DÙ	ēpišu (3-C)
DÙ	kalāma (5-A)
DÙ	kalû (ii) (2-B)
DÙ.A.BI	kalāma (5-A)
DU_6	tīlu (3-E)
DU_{11}.GA	qabû (2-B)
DUB	ṭuppu (7-F)
DUB.BI	ṭuppu (7-F)
DUG	ṭābu (3-C)
DUG.ŠAB	šappu
DÙG	muṭibbu (i) (10.6)
DÙG	ṭūbu (5-F)
DÙG.GA	ṭābtu (5-E)
DÙG.GA	ṭābu (3-C)
DÙG.GA	ṭūbu (5-F)
DUG_4.GA	qabû (2-B)
DUGUD	kabātu
DUGUD	kabtu (2-C)
DUL	katāmu (5-F)
DUL	tīlu (3-E)
DUMU	māru (1-A)
DUMU.MUNUS	mārtu (3-C)
DUNGU	urpatu (9-E)
E	īku
É	bītu (1-B)
É.AN.NA	ayyakku (10.8)
É.BAR	šangû (7-D)
É.GAL	ēkallu (1-B)
É.GAL.TUR.RA	egalturrû (9-A)
$É.GAR_8$	igāru (5-F)
É.KI.NÁ	bīt mayyāli

É.KUR	ēkurru (3-E)
É.PA.PAḪ	papāḫu (7-I)
É.SIG_4	igāru (5-F)
È	ṣītu (3-C)
E_{11}	elû (iii) (2-C)
EDIN	ṣēru (1-C)
ÉGI	rubātu
EGIR	warka (8-D)
EGIR	warki (3-B)
EGIR	warkītu (4-D)
EGIR	warkû (2-E)
EME	lišānu (6-D)
EME.GI_7	Šumeru
EN	adi (1-B)
EN	bēlu (1-A)
EN.NUN	maṣṣartu (7-G)
EN.NUN	maṣṣaru (10.13)
EN.TE.NA	kūṣu (9-F)
ÉNSI	iššiakku (2-A)
ÉR.ŠÀ.ḪUN.GÁ	eršaḫungû
EREN	erēnu (2-D)
ERIM	ṣābu (2-A)
ERIM	ummānu (1-C)
ERIM.TÁḪ	ne'rāru (10.7)
ESIR	kupru (7-D)
ESIR.UD.A	kupru (7-D)
EŠ.BAR	purussû (5-D)
ÈŠ.ÈŠ	eššēšu (10.8)
ÉŠ.GÀR	iškāru
EZEN	isinnu (6-E)
GA	šizbu
GÁ	šakānu (1-B)
GÁ.NA.MUŠEN	lurmu (10.10)
GÁ.NU_{11}.MUŠEN	lurmu (10.10)
GÁ.NUN	ganūnu (10.7)
GABA	irtu (4-E)
GABA	meḫretu (4-B)
GABA.DIB	gabadibbu (3-C)
GABA.RI	gabarû (9-D)
GABA.RI	māḫiru (5-E)
GABA.RI	meḫru (i) (10.11)

GADA	kitû (4-E)
GADA.MAḪ	gadamāḫu
GAG	sikkatu (5-A)
GAL	rabû (i) (1-A)
GÁL	bāšû (3-D)
GÁL	bašû (i) (3-A)
GAL_5.LÁ	gallû (9-B)
GALGA	milku (6-B)
GAR	šakānu (1-B)
GAR	šākinu (6-C)
GAR	šaknu (i) (4-C)
GAR.RA	uḫḫuzu (10.14)
GARZA	parṣu (4-E)
GAŠAN	bēltu (2-B)
GAZ	dâku (2-B)
GAZ	dīktu (3-B)
GAZ	ḫīpu (10.13)
GAZI.SAR	kasû (ii)
GE_6	mūšu (5-B)
GE_6	ṣalmu (i) (6-B)
GÉME	amtu
GÉŠ.U	nēr (7-D)
GEŠTU	uznu (4-D)
GI	qanû (5-D)
GI.AMBAR	appāru (6-C)
GI.DU_8	paṭīru
GI.DUB	gidubbû
GI.NA	kīnu (3-D)
GI_6	mūšu (5-B)
GIBIL	edēšu (2-C)
GIBIL	eššu (10.13)
GÍBIL	maqlūtu (10.14)
GÍBIL	qalû (ii) (10.14)
GÍBIL	qilûtu (6-F)
GÍBIL	šarāpu (3-A)
GÍD	arāku (4-E)
GÍD	mūraku (10.8)
GÍD.DA	arāku (4-E)
GÍD.DA	arku (8-C)
GÍD.DA	mūraku (10.8)
GIDIM	eṭemmu (10.6)

GIG	marṣiš (8-B)
GIG	marṣu (3-D)
GIG	murṣu (10.12)
GIM	kīma (1-C)
GIN	kânu (2-A)
GIN	kīnu (3-D)
GÍN	šiqlu (7-A)
GÍR	patru (5-D)
GÍR.AN.BAR	patru (5-D)
GÍR.TAB	zuqiqīpu (10.9)
GÍR.TAB.LÚ.U_{18}.LU	girtablilu
GÍR.TUR	uṣultu
GÌR	šēpu (1-C)
GÌR.ARAD	šakkanakku (2-E)
GÌR.BAL	riḫṣu (10.14)
GÌR.PAD.DA	eṣemtu (7-H)
GÌR.PAD.DU	eṣemtu (7-H)
GISKIM	ittu (ii) (8-E)
GIŠ	iṣu (4-C)
GIŠ.APIN	epinnu (10.10)
GIŠ.AŠ.TE	kussû (2-A)
GIŠ.AŠ.TI	kussû (2-A)
GIŠ.BA.AN.DU_8.DU_8	banduddû
GIŠ.BAL	pilaqqu
GIŠ.BANŠUR	paššuru (7-A)
^{d}GIŠ.BAR	gīru (3-B)
GIŠ.DÌḪ	baltu (10.10)
GIŠ.DÍLIM	itqūru
GIŠ.DUN_4	nīru (2-B)
GIŠ.ESI	ušû (4-A)
GIŠ.GADA	kitû (4-E)
GIŠ.GAG.U_4.TAG.GA	šiltāḫu (8-A)
GIŠ.GAN	kannu (10.10)
GIŠ.GAN.DU_7	ḫittu (10.12)
GIŠ.GEŠTIN	karānu (4-A)
GIŠ.GEŠTIN.GÍR	amurdinnu
GIŠ.GI	apu (9-A)
GIŠ.GI	qanû (5-D)
GIŠ.GIDRU	ḫaṭṭu (4-D)
GIŠ.GIGIR	narkabtu (2-A)
GIŠ.GÍR	patru (5-D)

GIŠ.GÌR.GUB	gištappu (10.6)
GIŠ.GIŠ	nīru (2-B)
GIŠ.GIŠIMMAR	gišimmaru (10.10)
GIŠ.GU.ZA	kussû (2-A)
GIŠ.GUB	zaqāpu (4-C)
GIŠ.GURUN	inbu (5-F)
GIŠ.GUŠUR	gušūru (3-D)
GIŠ.ḪA.LU.ÚB	ḫaluppu
GIŠ.ḪA.ŠUR	ḫašūru (10.9)
GIŠ.ḪAŠḪUR	ḫašḫūru
GIŠ.ḪAŠḪUR	ḫašūru (10.9)
GIŠ.ḪUR	gišḫurru (9-D)
GIŠ.ḪUR	uṣurtu (9-A)
GIŠ.IG	daltu (4-B)
GIŠ.IN.NU	tibnu (8-D)
GIŠ.KAK.TI	ūṣu (9-C)
GIŠ.KÌM	ḫilēpu
GIŠ.KIN.GEŠTIN	isḫunnatu
GIŠ.KIRI$_6$	kirû (4-D)
GIŠ.KIRI$_6$.MAḪ	kirimaḫḫu (8-C)
GIŠ.KIŠI$_{16}$	ašāgu (10.9)
GIŠ.KU.AN	miṭṭu (10.6)
GIŠ.LÁ	tuqumtu (5-C)
GIŠ.LAL	ṣimittu (5-A)
GIŠ.LAL	tuqumtu (5-C)
GIŠ.LE.U$_5$.UM	lē'u (10.7)
GIŠ.LI	burāšu (5-D)
GIŠ.MÁ	eleppu (4-E)
GIŠ.MÁ.GU.LA	magulû (10.6)
GIŠ.MÁ.KAN.NA	musukkannu (3-E)
GIŠ.MAR	marru (ii) (10.8)
GIŠ.MAR.GÍD.DA	ereqqu (10.10)
GIŠ.MAR.ŠE.RA.AḪ	narpasu
GIŠ.MES.MÁ.KAN	musukkannu (3-E)
GIŠ.MI	ṣillu (9-E)
GIŠ.NÁ	eršu (iv) (5-D)
GIŠ.NA$_5$	pitnu (10.8)
GIŠ.NÍG.GIDRU	ḫaṭṭu (4-D)
GIŠ.NÍG.TUKU	gišimmaru (10.10)
GIŠ.NU.ÚR.MA	nurmû
GIŠ.NU.ÚR.MA	kuduppānu

GIŠ.PAN	qaštu (3-C)
GIŠ.PÈŠ	tittu
GIŠ.SÙH̰.NA	šaššūgu
GIŠ.ŠENNUR.BABBAR.RA	kamiššaru
GIŠ.ŠIBIR	šibirru (8-D)
GIŠ.ŠIM.GAM.MA	ṣumlalû
GIŠ.ŠIM.GIG	kanaktu
GIŠ.ŠIM.LI	burāšu (5-D)
GIŠ.ŠIM.ŠAL	šimiššalû
GIŠ.ŠUB.BA	isqu (7-G)
GIŠ.ŠUDUN	nīru (2-B)
GIŠ.ŠUR.MÌN	šurmēnu (3-E)
GIŠ.TIR	qištu (6-F)
GIŠ.TÚG	taskarinnu (3-E)
GIŠ.TUKUL	kakku (1-C)
GIŠ.TUKUL.DINGIR	miṭṭu (10.6)
GIŠ.Ù.SUB	nalbanu (10.13)
GIŠ.Ù.ŠUB	nalbattu (10.5)
GIŠ.Ù.SUH̰$_5$	ašūh̰u (10.9)
GIŠ.ÙR	gušūru (3-D)
GIŠ.UŠ.BAR	ušparu (10.7)
GIŠ.UŠBAR$_5$	ušparu (10.7)
GIŠ.ZÀ.MÍ	sammû (10.7)
GIŠ.ZU	lēʾu (10.7)
GÌŠ	birku (7-G)
GIŠKIM	ittu (ii) (8-E)
GU	qû (i) (9-E)
GU.AN.NA	ešmarû (8-C)
GÚ.GAL	gugallu (7-G)
GÚ.UN	biltu (2-A)
GÚ.ZI	kāsu
GÙ.SUM	mih̰iṣtu
GU$_4$	alpu (2-A)
GU$_4$.ÁB	arh̰u (ii)
GU$_4$.AM	rīmu (5-C)
GU$_4$.AMAR	būru (ii) (10.9)
GU$_4$.MAH̰	gumāh̰u (10.14)
GU$_4$.NÍTA	alpu (2-A)
GUB	izuzzu (2-B)
GUB	nazuzzu
GÙB	šumēla (7-E)

GÙB	šumēlu (10.13)
GUKKAL	kukkallu
GUN	biltu (2-A)
GÙN	birmu (4-C)
GUR	kurru
GUR	târu (1-C)
GÚR	kanšu (4-A)
GÚR	kippatu (9-D)
GURUN	inbu (5-F)
ḪÁD.A	ablu
ḪAR	šawiru (7-D)
ḪE.GÁL	ḫengallu (5-F)
ḪÉ.NUN	nuḫšu (5-F)
ḪI.A	mādu (2-D)
ḪI.A	ummānu (1-C)
ḪI.LI	kuzbu (7-H)
ḪUL	lemnu (4-C)
ḪUL	lumnu (10.10)
ḪUL	pašqu (5-F)
ḪÚL	ḫadîš (4-B)
ḪÚL	ḫidiātu (6-A)
ḪUŠ	ezzu (4-D)
ḪUŠ	ruššû (6-A)
ḪUŠ.A	ruššû (6-A)
Ì	šamnu (3-B)
Ì.BUR	šaman pūri
Ì.DU_8.GAL	idugallu
Ì.GIŠ	šamnu (3-B)
Ì.NUN	ḫimētu (9-B)
Ì.SAG	rūštu (10.13)
IBILA	aplu (6-F)
ÍD	nārtu (i) (9-G)
ÍD	nāru (i) (3-D)
ÍD.ḪAL.ḪAL	Idiqlatiš
IDIM	nagbu (5-B)
IGI	amāru (2-B)
IGI	maḫāru (2-A)
IGI	meḫretu (4-B)
IGI	pāna (5-E)
IGI	pānu (1-C)
IGI.BAR	palāsu (4-B)

IGI.DU$_8$.A	tāmartu (3-D)
IGI.GÁL	igigallu (10.5)
IGI.II	īnu (3-C)
IGI.KÁ	barû (ii)
IGI.LÁ	amāru (2-B)
IGI.LAL	tāmartu (3-D)
IGI.SÁ	igisû (6-D)
ÍGIRA.MUŠEN	igirû (10.14)
IKU	ikû (10.5)
ÍL	našû (ii) (2-E)
ILLAT	illatu (5-F)
ILLAT	tillatu (10.10)
ILLU	mīlu (4-C)
IM	šāru (i) (6-D)
IM	ṭīdu (10.14)
IM.BABBAR	gaṣṣu
^{d}IM.DUGUD.MUŠEN	anzû (8-E)
IM.GÍD.DA	liginnu
IM.KUR.RA	šadû (ii) (9-E)
IM.LÍMMU.BA	šārī erbetti
IM.MAR.TU	amurru (10.14)
IM.RI.A	kimtu (6-A)
IM.SI.SÁ	ištānu (8-B)
IM.SIG$_7$.SIG$_7$	dāmātu
IM.U$_{18}$.LU	šūtu (ii) (8-E)
^{d}INANNA	ištaru (4-C)
INIM	awātu (3-B)
INIM.GAR	egerrû (10.9)
ÌR	wardu (3-D)
^{d}IŠ.TAR	ištaru (4-C)
ITI	urḫu (4-D)
ITI	warḫu (4-B)
ITI.BAD.KÁ	pīt bābi (10.6)
IZI	išātu (2-D)
KA	pû (ii)
KA.DU$_8$.Ù.DA	pīt pî (10.5)
KA.DU$_8$.UD.DA	pīt pî (10.5)
KA.KEŠDA	kiṣru (4-A)
KA.LUḪ.Ù.DA	mīs pî (10.6)
KA.LUḪ.UD.DA	mīs pî (10.6)
KÁ	bābu (2-B)

KÁ.GAL	abullu (2-E)
KA_5.A	šēlebu
KAL	dannatu (4-C)
KAL	dannu (1-B)
KAL	dannūtu (3-C)
KALA	dannu (1-B)
KALAG	danānu (ii) (4-A)
KALAM	mātu (1-A)
KAM	erēšu (ii) (7-H)
KAR	ekēmu (3-C)
KAR	kāru (7-A)
KASKAL	gerru (2-B)
KASKAL	ḫarrānu (3-C)
KASKAL.GÍD	bēru (iii) (4-C)
KARAŠ	karāšu (4-B)
KAŠ	šikaru (7-G)
KAŠ.MAḪ	kašmaḫḫu
KAŠ.SAG	šikaru (7-G)
$KAŠ_4$	lismu
KI	ašru (1-C)
KI	erṣetu (2-C)
KI	itti (1-B)
KI.GAL	kigallu (9-F)
KI.GUB	mazzāzu (5-F)
KI.ḪUL	kiḫullû
KI.LÁ	šuqultu (6-C)
KI.LAM	maḫīru (8-F)
KI.MAḪ	kimaḫḫu (8-F)
KI.MIN	šanîš (10.10)
KI.NÁ	mayyālu (9-F)
KI.NE	kinūnu (10.11)
KI.SAG	kaspu (1-C)
KI.SIKIL	wardatu (10.5)
KI.ṢIR	kiṣru (4-A)
KI.TA	šaplītu
KI.TA	šaplû (4-D)
KI.TA	šaplu (ii) (7-B)
KI.TA	šupālû (10.8)
KI.TUŠ	šubtu (2-B)
KÌD.KÌD	kikiṭṭû
KIN	šipru (2-A)

KISAL	kisallu (6-A)
KISAL.MAḪ	kisalmāḫu (10.5)
KIŠ	kiṣru (4-A)
KIŠ	kiššatu (1-B)
KIŠIB	rittu (5-C)
KÚ	akālu (5-G)
KÙ	ellu (3-B)
KÙ	peṣû (4-E)
KÙ.BABBAR	kaspu (1-C)
KÙ.GI	ḫurāṣu (1-C)
KU$_4$	erēbu (2-A)
KU$_6$	nūnu (6-E)
KU$_6$.LÚ.U$_{18}$.LU	kulīlu
KUD	nakāsu (3-A)
KUD	niksu (6-C)
KUD	parāsu (5-A)
KUD	pārisu (9-G)
KUN	zibbatu
KUN$_4$	askuppu (5-D)
KUR	kašādu (1-B)
KUR	kišittu (3-A)
KUR	mātu (1-A)
KUR	napāḫu (9-A)
KUR	šadû (i) (1-B)
KUR.GI	kurkû (10.9)
KUR.GI.MUŠEN	kurkû (10.9)
KUR.NU.GI$_4$.A	Kurnugi
KÚR	nakāru (3-A)
KÚR	nakru (i) (6-F)
KURUN.NAM	kurunnu (8-F)
KUŠ	mašku (4-D)
KUŠ.DA.E.SIR	mešēnu
KUŠ.DUḪ.ŠI.A	dušû (10.11)
KUŠ.E.SÍR	šēnu
KUŠ.PA	appatu (10.8)
KUŠ.ÙMMU	nādu (i) (10.9)
KÙŠ	ammatu (3-D)
LAL	maṭû
LAL	šaqû (i) (4-E)
LAL	tarāṣu (4-B)
LAL	tarṣu (4-D)

LÀL	dišpu (8-H)
dLAMMA	lamassu (4-E)
LI.LI.ÌZ	lilissu
LIBIR.RA	labīru (6-B)
LIM	līm (2-A)
LIM-A.A	līmâ
LÍMMU	arbaʾu (5-C)
LÍMMU	erbe (2-D)
LÚ	awīlu (5-D)
LÚ	ša (i) (1-A)
LÚ.2	šanû (ii) (5-A)
LÚ.2	šanû (i) (5-G)
LÚ.3.U_5	tašlīšu (10.10)
LÚ.A KIN	mār šipri (9-A)
LÚ.A.BA	ṭupšarru (7-H)
LÚ.A.ZU	asû
LÚ.AB.BA	šību (10.8)
LÚ.ÀD	pagru (4-B)
LÚ.AGRIG	abarakku
LÚ.AGRIG	mašennu
LÚ.ARAD	wardu (3-D)
LÚ.AŠGAB	aškāpu
LÚ.DAB	mukillu (7-D)
LÚ.DAM.GÀR	tamkāru
LÚ.DUB.SAR	ṭupšarru (7-H)
LÚ.EDIN	ṣīru (ii) (7-B)
LÚ.EN GIŠ.GIGIR.MEŠ	bēl narkabti (8-A)
LÚ.EN.NAM	bēl pīḫāti (3-C)
LÚ.EN.NAM	pīḫātu (2-C)
LÚ.EN.URU	bēl āli (5-A)
LÚ.ENGAR	ikkaru
LÚ.ERIM	ṣābu (2-A)
LÚ.GAL	rabû (i) (1-A)
LÚ.GAL	rubû (2-A)
LÚ.GAL.BI.LUL	rab-šāqê (10.8)
LÚ.GAL.GI.BÙR	rab ṭupšarri
LÚ.GAL.KAR	rab kāri
LÚ.GALA	kalû (iii) (9-H)
LÚ.GAR	šaknu (ii) (2-B)
LÚ.GAR.KUR	šakin māti (6-A)
LÚ.GÍD.DA	šaddidu

LÚ.GÌR.NITA	šakkanakku (2-E)
LÚ.GIŠ.DA	aʾlu (10.6)
LÚ.GIŠ.GIGIR	awīl narkabti
LÚ.GÚ.EN.NA	šandabakku (9-A)
LÚ.GURUŠ	eṭlu (4-C)
LÚ.GURUŠ.TUR	batūlu (10.13)
LÚ.ḪAL	bārû (9-D)
LÚ.Ì.DU_8	atûtu
LÚ.KA.PIRIG	wāšipu (10.10)
LÚ.KA.PÌRIG	wāšipu (10.10)
LÚ.KA.ṢIR	kāṣiru (9-H)
LÚ.KAL.LAP	kallāpu (10.9)
LÚ.KIN.GI_4.A	mār šipri (9-A)
LÚ.KÙ.DÍM	kutīmu
LÚ.KU_4	ēribu (10.8)
LÚ.KÚR	nakru (ii) (2-A)
LÚ.LÚNGA	sīrāšû (10.7)
LÚ.MÁ.$LAḪ_5$	malāḫu
LÚ.MAḪ	ṣīru (ii) (7-B)
LÚ.MAŠ.MAŠ	wāšipu (10.10)
LÚ.MUḪALDIM	nuḫatimmu
LÚ.MUŠ.$LAḪ_4$	mušlalaḫḫu
LÚ.NAGAR	nagāru (10.5)
LÚ.NAM	pīḫātu (2-C)
LÚ.NAR	nāru (ii) (6-B)
LÚ.NAR.GAL	nargallu
LÚ.NIGIR	nāgiru (7-I)
LÚ.NIMGIR	nāgiru (7-I)
LÚ.NU.ÈŠ	nêšakku (9-I)
LÚ.NU.GIŠ.$KIRI_6$	nukaribbu (10.6)
LÚ.RA.GABA	rakbû (6-B)
LÚ.SAG	ša reši
LÚ.SAG	šūt rēši (2-C)
LÚ.SAG.KAL	ašarēdu (4-D)
LÚ.SANGA	šangû (7-D)
LÚ.SIMUG	nappāḫu
LÚ.SIPA	rēʾû (4-A)
LÚ.SUKKAL	šukkallu (7-D)
LÚ.SUKKAL.MAḪ	sukkalmaḫḫu
LÚ.ŠÀ.TAM	šatammu (10.7)
LÚ.ŠÁMAN.LÁ	šamallû

LÚ.ŠEŠ.GAL	šešgallūtu
LÚ.ŠID	iššiakku (2-A)
LÚ.ŠITIM.GAL	šitimgallu (10.11)
LÚ.ŠU.GI	šību (10.8)
LÚ.ŠU.KU_6	bāʾeru
LÚ.TIL.GÍD	qīpu (5-G)
LÚ.TIRUM	tīru (10.14)
LÚ.TÚG.KAL	mukabbû
LÚ.TUR	ṣuḫāru
LÚ.UKU.UŠ	rēdû (10.8)
LÚ.UŠ	rēdû (10.8)
LUGAL	šarru (1-A)
LUGUD	šarku
MA.NA	manû (iv) (2-B)
MA.SÁ.AB	masabbu (10.9)
MAḪ	ṣīru (i) (2-A)
MAN	šanû (ii) (5-A)
MAN	šarru (1-A)
MAR	zarû (10.6)
MAŠ.DÀ	ṣabītu (9-C)
MAŠ.EN.GAG	muškēnu
MAŠ.KÁN	maškanu (6-E)
MAŠ.MAŠ	mašmaššu
MAŠ.TAB.BA	māšu (10.14)
MÁŠ	ṣibtu (ii) (10.5)
MÁŠ	ṣibtu (i) (10.11)
MÁŠ.ANŠE	būlu (7-E)
MÁŠ.GE_6	šuttu (6-D)
MÁŠ.GI_6	šuttu (6-D)
MÁŠ.ŠU.GÍD.GÍD	bārû (9-D)
MAŠKIM	rābiṣu (10.6)
MÁŠKIM	rābiṣu (10.6)
ME	meʾatu (1-C)
ME.LÁM	melemmu (4-A)
MÈ	tāḫāzu (2-A)
MU	nīšu (ii) (7-H)
MU	šattu (3-B)
MU	šuāti (2-A)
MU	šumu (1-B)
MU	zakāru (3-E)
MU	zikru (2-C)

MU.AN.NA	šattišamma (4-B)
MU.DIŠ.KÁM	šattišamma (4-B)
MU.SAR	mušarû (2-D)
MU.SAR	mūšaru (10.7)
MÚD	dāmu (5-A)
MUL	kakkabu (8-C)
MUL.AL.LUL	alluttu
MUL.APIN	epinnu (10.10)
MUL.MAR.GÍD.DA	ereqqu (10.10)
MUL.PAN	qaštu (3-C)
MUN	ṭabtu (7-G)
MUN	ṭābtu (5-E)
$MUNU_4$	buqlu (10.10)
MUNUS	sinništu (5-B)
MUNUS.ÁB.ZA.ZA	apsasû (5-B)
MUNUS.AGRIG	abarakkatu
MUNUS.AGRIG	abarakkūtu (7-B)
MUNUS.AMA	ummu (i) (5-E)
MUNUS.ANŠE.EDIN.NA	serremtu
MUNUS.ANŠE.KUR.RA	urītu (10.5)
MUNUS.DUMU	mārtu (3-C)
MUNUS.É.GAL	ša ēkalli (6-A)
MUNUS.ERIM	sekretu (6-A)
MUNUS.ERIM.É.GAL	sekret ēkalli (8-B)
MUNUS.ḪUL	lemuttu (3-D)
MUNUS.KAL.TUR	batultu (10.11)
MUNUS.KALA	dannatu (4-C)
MUNUS.KUR	ša ēkalli (6-A)
MUNUS.KÚR	nukurtu (10.5)
MUNUS.ᵈLAMMA	lamassu (4-E)
MUNUS.NAR	nārtu (ii) (7-G)
MUNUS.NIN	aḫātu (8-C)
$MUNUS.SIG_5$	damqu (2-E)
MUNUS.ŠÀ.É.GAL	ša ēkalli (6-A)
$MURU_9$	imbaru (7-A)
$MURUB_4$	qabaltu (7-B)
$MURUB_4$	qablû (10.10)
$MURUB_4$	qablu (ii) (3-D)
$MURUB_4$	qablu (i) (2-D)
MUŠ	ṣerru (i) (10.14)
MUŠ.ḪUŠ	mušḫuššu

MUŠEN	iṣṣūru (4-C)
MUŠEN.UZ	ūsu (ii)
NA.GADA	nāqidūtu
NA$_4$	abnu (2-E)
NA$_4$.AD.BAR	atbaru (10.5)
NA$_4$.AŠ.GÌ.GÌ	ašgigû (10.9)
NA$_4$.BABBAR.DILI	pappardaliu (7-C)
NA$_4$.BABBAR.MIN$_5$	papparmīnu (10.6)
NA$_4$.DAG.GAZ	takkassu (10.11)
NA$_4$.DÚR.MI.NA	turminû (10.5)
NA$_4$.DÚR.MI.NA.BÀN.DA	turminabandû (6-C)
NA$_4$.EN.GI.SA$_6$	engisû
NA$_4$.GI.RIM.ḪI.LI.BA	girim ḫilibê (10.6)
NA$_4$.GI.RIM.ḪI.LI.BA	ḫilibû (10.6)
NA$_4$.GIRIM.ḪI.LI.BA.	girim ḫilibê (10.6)
NA$_4$.GIŠ.NU.GAL	ašnugallu (4-B)
NA$_4$.GIŠ.NU$_{11}$.GAL	ašnugallu (4-B)
NA$_4$.GÚ	kišādu (4-A)
NA$_4$.GUG	sāmtu (10.13)
NA$_4$.KA.GI.NA.	ḫusāru
NA$_4$.KIŠIB	kunukku (8-E)
NA$_4$.KUN$_4$	askuppu (5-D)
NA$_4$.MUŠ.GÍR	muššāru (10.11)
NA$_4$.NA.RÚ	narû (2-D)
NA$_4$.NA.RÚ.A	narû (2-D)
NA$_4$.NÍR	ḫulālu
NA$_4$.PA	ayyartu
NA$_4$.SAG.GIL.MUD	sangilimud (10.5)
NA$_4$.^{d}ŠE.TIR	pendû (9-E)
NA$_4$.ŠIM.BI.ZI.DA.	guḫlu (9-A)
NA$_4$.ZA.GÌN	uqnû (5-B)
NA$_4$.ZA.GÌN.DURU$_5$	zagiddurû
NA$_4$.ZÚ	ṣurru (ii) (8-E)
NA$_4$.ZÚ	šinnu (3-D)
NA$_4$.ZÚ.MAŠ.DÀ	šinni ṣabīti (10.6)
NA$_5$	pitnu (10.8)
NAG	šaqû (iii) (9-C)
NAM	annû (3-B)
NAM	šīmtu (3-B)
^{d}NAM	šīmtu (3-B)
NAM.TI.LA	balāṭu (i) (2-E)

NAM.ÚŠ.MEŠ	mūtānu (10.10)
NENNI	annanna (10.7)
NÍ	ramānu (3-C)
NÍ.GI	ḫammāʾu (10.12)
NIDBA	nindabû (8-D)
NÍG.BA	qiāšu (4-A)
NÍG.BA	qīštu (7-E)
NÍG.BÚN.NA.KU$_6$	šeleppû
NÍG.DU	kudurru (i) (6-E)
NÍG.È	lītu (i) (3-D)
NÍG.GA	makkūru (2-E)
NÍG.GIG	ikkibu (7-H)
NÍG.GIG	maruṣtu (9-B)
NÍG.GUL	akkullu (7-C)
NÍG.KA$_9$	nikkassu
NÍG.NA	nignakku (10.7)
NÍG.SA.SA	mutḫummu (10.6)
NÍG.ŠU	būšu (2-D)
NIGA	marû (i) (8-A)
NIGIN	napḫaru (3-A)
NIGIN	nasḫuru
NIGIN	siḫirtu (2-C)
NIM	zubbu
NIM.GÍR	berqu (9-A)
NIN	bēltu (2-B)
^{d}NIN.KILIM	šikkû (10.8)
NIN$_9$	aḫātu (8-C)
NINDA	akalu (8-A)
NINDA	nindanu (7-G)
NINDU	tinūru
NIR.GÁL	etellu (7-H)
NITA	zikaru (3-E)
NÍTA	zikaru (3-E)
NU	lā (1-A)
NU	ṣalmu (ii) (2-C)
NUMUN	zēru (ii) (2-C)
NUN	rubû (2-A)
NUNDUM	šaptu (5-C)
NUNUZ	pelû
NUNUZ	perʾu (6-A)
PA$_5$	palgu (10.9)

PAP	aḫu (i) (2-D)
PAP	napḫaru (3-A)
PAP	naṣāru (4-B)
PAP	nāṣiru (4-E)
PAP.ḪAL	pušqu (10.10)
PÉŠ.GIŠ.GI	ušummu
PI	parsiktu
PIRIG.GAL	piriggallu (10.14)
PISAN	pišannu
PÚ	būrtu (8-B)
RE.É.UM	rē'û (4-A)
RÉM	rēmēnû (7-H)
RU	šeriktu (6-E)
SÁ	šanānu (4-B)
SÁ.DUG$_4$	sattukku (5-B)
SA$_5$	malû (i) (5-G)
SA$_5$	sāmu (10.9)
SAG	pūtu (3-E)
SAG	rēštu (6-E)
SAG	rēštû (6-A)
SAG	rēšu (2-A)
SAG.DIN	ṭēmu (3-D)
SAG.DU	qaqqadu (3-A)
SAG.GE$_6$.GA.A	ṣalmāt-qaqqadi
SAG.KAL	ašarēdu (4-D)
SAG.KAL	ašarettu
SAG.KI	pūtu (3-E)
SAG.KUL	sikkūru
SAGŠU	kubšu
SAḪAR	eperu (5-C)
SAḪAR.ŠUB.BA	saḫaršubbû
SANTAK$_4$	santakku
SAR	mūšaru (10.7)
SAR	šaṭru (3-C)
SAR	šiṭru (2-D)
SI	qarnu (9-E)
SI.GAR	šigaru (5-F)
SI.SÁ	ešēru (3-A)
SIG	damqu (2-E)
SIG	enšu (7-I)
SÍG	šīpātu (8-B)

SÍG.ZA.GÌN	uqnû (5-B)
SÍG.ZA.GÌN.MI	argamannu (6-C)
SÍG.ZA.GÌN.MI	takiltu (6-F)
SÍG.ZA.GÌN.SA_5	argamannu (6-C)
SÌG	maḫāṣu (2-E)
SIG_4	libittu (4-B)
SIG_4.AL.ÙR.RA	agurru (4-C)
SIG_5	damqu (2-E)
SIG_5	dumqu (5-E)
SIG_5	libittu (4-B)
SIG_7	warqu
SÍK	šīpātu (8-B)
SILA	sūqu (7-A)
SÌLA	qû (ii)
SILA.DAGAL.LA	rebītu (6-F)
SILIM	šalāmu (ii) (3-E)
SILIM	šalāmu (i) (10.6)
SILIM	šulmu (3-B)
SISKUR	nīqu (2-E)
SÍSKUR	nīqu (2-E)
SU	zumru (8-E)
SÙ	rūqu (2-C)
SÙ	ṭebû (9-A)
SUḪ	uššu (2-C)
SUḪUR	ṭēḫu (7-I)
SUḪUR.MÁŠ.KU_6	suḫurmāšu
SUḪUŠ	išdu (5-A)
SUM	nadānu (ii) (3-A)
SUM	qiāšu (4-A)
SUM.MU	nadnu (10.6)
SUMUN	labīru (6-B)
SÚR.DÙ.MUŠEN	surdû
ŠÀ	libbu (1-B)
ŠÀ.BAL.BAL	līpu (5-F)
ŠÀ.GI.$GURU_6$	šagigurrû (10.10)
ŠÀ.GI.$GURU_6$.A	šagigurrû (10.10)
ŠÀ.TÙR	šassūru (10.8)
ŠAḪ	šaḫû (7-H)
ŠÁM	šīmu
ŠANABI	šinipu
ŠAPRA	šabrû (i)

ŠÁR	kiššatu (1-B)
ŠÁR	šār (6-F)
$ŠAR_5$	šār (6-F)
ŠE	marû (i) (8-A)
ŠE	û (6-A)
ŠE	û (6-A)
ŠE	uṭṭatu (10.14)
ŠE.AM	û (6-A)
ŠE.BAR	uṭṭatu (10.14)
ŠE.BÙLUG.MEŠ	buqlu (10.10)
ŠE.GA	magāru (5-G)
ŠE.GA	migru (4-A)
ŠE.GA	mitgāru (10.13)
ŠE.GA	šemû (2-A)
ŠE.GIG	kibtu
ŠE.GIŠ.Ì	šamaššammū
ŠE.IM	û (6-A)
ŠE.IN.NU	tibnu (8-D)
ŠE.KIN.TAR	eṣēdu (i) (10.6)
$ŠE.MUNU_4$	buqlu (10.10)
ŠE.NUMUN	zēru (ii) (2-C)
ŠE.PAD	û (6-A)
ŠE.PAD	uṭṭatu (10.14)
ŠE.PAD.LIM	šeʾu (10.7)
ŠE.UM	šeʾu (10.7)
ŠÈG	zunnu (6-E)
ŠEŠ	aḫḫūtu (10.5)
ŠEŠ	aḫu (i) (2-D)
ŠEŠ	annû (3-B)
^{d}ŠEŠ.KI	nannāru (8-G)
ŠÉŠ	pašāšu (4-A)
ŠID	iššiakkūtu (10.14)
ŠID	manûtu
ŠIM	rīqu (5-A)
ŠIM.EN.DI	suādu
ŠIM.LI	burāšu (5-D)
ŠIM.SES	murru
ŠU	gāmilu (10.13)
ŠU	qātu (1-B)
ŠU.ÍL.KÁM	šuʾillakku
ŠU.KA.AN	siparru (2-D)

ŠU.NIGIN	napḫaru (3-A)
ŠU.NÍGIN	napḫaru (3-A)
ŠU.SI	ubānu (5-D)
ŠÚ	erbu (ii) (6-C)
ŠÚ	kiššatu (1-B)
ŠUB	nadû (i) (5-B)
ŠUB	nadû (iii) (2-B)
ŠÙD	ikribu (3-B)
ŠÙD	karābu (5-F)
TA	ištu (1-B)
TA	itti (1-B)
TAG	liptu (7-B)
TÁR.KÍL	tarkullu
TE	lētu (10.14)
TE	ṭeḫû (8-B)
TÉŠ	bāštu (8-A)
TI	balāṭu (i) (2-E)
TI	balṭu (5-B)
TI	leqû (3-C)
TI.LA	balāṭu (i) (2-E)
TI.LA	balṭu (5-B)
TI_8.MUŠEN	erû (i) (8-H)
TIBIRA	qurqurru
TIL	gamru (10.5)
TIL	labīru (6-B)
TIN	balāṭu (i) (2-E)
^{d}TIR.AN.NA	manziat (10.5)
TU.KUR_4.MUŠEN	sukannīnu
TU.MUŠEN	summatu (10.5)
TU.RA	marṣu (3-D)
TÚG	ṣubātu (10.13)
TÚG.GADA	kitû (4-E)
TÚG.GÚ.È	naḫlaptu
TÚG.SAGŠU	kubšu
TÚG.SÍG	sissiktu
TUK	išû (i) (3-A)
TUK	rašû (3-D)
TUKU	išû (i) (3-A)
TÙM	tabālu (7-I)
TUR	ṣeḫru (ii) (7-D)
TUR	ṣeḫru (i) (3-A)

TÙR	tarbaṣu (10.13)
ᵈU.DAR	ištaru (4-C)
Ú	annû (3-B)
Ú	šammu (9-E)
Ú.GAMUN	kamūnu (i)
Ú.LAL	ašqulālu
Ú.SAR	warqu
Ú.SUM.SAR	šūmū
Ú.SUM.SIKIL.SAR	šamaškillu
Ú.ZAG.ḪI.LI	saḫliu (10.12)
Ú.ZAG.ḪI.LI.SAR	saḫliu (10.12)
Ù	annû (3-B)
U_4.GAL	ugallu
U_4.ḪUL.GÁL.E	uḫulgallu
U_4.SAKAR	uskāru
U_5	rakābu (6-B)
U_6.NIR	ziqqurratu (5-G)
U_8	gurrutu
U_8	ṣēnu (iii) (2-C)
UB	kibru (2-B)
UBARA	kidinnu (8-E)
UD	inūma (2-D)
UD	ūmu (i) (1-B)
UD	ūmu (ii) (10.7)
UD.DA	ṣētu
UD.ÈŠ.ÈŠ	ūm eššēši
UDU	immeru (3-C)
UDU.NIM	ḫurāpu
UDU.NÍTA	immeru (3-C)
UDU.SILA$_4$	puḫādu
UDU.SISKUR	nīqu (2-E)
UDU.SÍSKUR	nīqu (2-E)
UDUN	utūnu (10.14)
UGU	eli (1-B)
UGU	muḫḫu (2-C)
UGULA	waklu (7-H)
UKKIN	puḫru (5-A)
UM.ME.A	ummiānu (5-F)
UMUN	bēlu (1-A)
UMUŠ	ṭēmu (3-D)
UN	nišu (1-B)

UR.BAR.RA	barbaru
UR.GI$_7$	kalbu (9-F)
UR.IDIM	uridimmu
UR.MAḪ	nēšu (6-B)
UR.MAḪ	urmaḫḫu (6-D)
UR.SAG	qarrādu (6-F)
UR.SAG	qurādu (3-E)
ÚR	išdu (5-A)
ÙR	ūru
UR$_5$	šuāti (2-A)
^{d}ÙRI.GAL	urigallu (9-G)
URU	ālu (1-A)
URU.AN.ZA.GÀR	dimtu (i) (8-H)
URU.ḪAL.ṢU.MEŠ	birtu (i) (3-D)
URUDU	werû (2-D)
ÚS.SA.DU	šiddu (3-C)
US$_5$.UDU	ṣēnu (iii) (2-C)
UŠ	šiddu (3-C)
UŠ	šūši (4-E)
ÚŠ	dāmu (5-A)
ÚŠ	mītu
ÚŠ	mūtu (7-E)
ÚŠ.MEŠ	mūtānu (10.10)
UŠ$_8$	uššu (2-C)
UŠUMGAL	ušumgallu (8-A)
^{d}UTU	šamšu (3-A)
UTUL	utullu (9-E)
ÚTUL	diqāru (5-D)
UZ.MUŠEN	ūsu (ii)
UZ.TUR.MUŠEN	paspasu (10.7)
UZU	šīru (4-E)
UZU.ÉLLAG	kalītu
UZU.ME.ZÉ	isu
UZU.UR$_5$.ÚŠ	têrtu (8-G)
ZA.GÌN	uqnû (5-B)
ZA.ZA	apsasû (5-B)
ZABAR	siparru (2-D)
ZAG	imitta
ZAG	imna (8-A)
ZAG	imnu (10.10)
ZAG	pāṭu (2-D)

ZÁḪ	ḫalāqu (3-A)
ZÁLAG	munawwiru (10.14)
ZÁLAG	nawāru (4-A)
ZÁLAG	nūru (6-F)
ZI	dekû (2-D)
ZI	napištu (2-B)
ZI	nasāḫu (3-C)
ZI	tebû (4-B)
ZI	tību (4-C)
ZÌ.DA	qēmu
ZÍB	teleʾû
ZU.AB	apsû (6-C)
ZÚ	šinnu (3-D)
ZÚ AM.SI	šinni pīri (5-F)
ZÚ.LUM.MA	suluppu (9-C)

APPENDIX E: LOGOGRAM LIST 2 (AKKADIAN-SUMERIAN)

In this appendix you will find a near-exhaustive list of logographic writings arranged alphabetically by their Akkadian equivalents (see appendix D for a broader introduction to the logographic writing system). Each Akkadian word will be followed by the list in which it appears in chapters 1–10 of this book. When no list is provided, this indicates that the word occurs fewer than five times in the Assyrian royal inscription corpus.

This appendix is meant to serve two functions. First, it allows coordination with the lists in the main body of this book. In those lists, any word that has a logographic writing is presented in **bold**. This indicates that the student can come to this appendix in order to see the logographic writings of that word. Students may want to learn these writings along with the meaning of the Akkadian word or may want to make such a task a separate endeavor.

The second purpose of this list is to enable you to see all of the logographic writings possible for a given word at a glance. Many words have multiple possible logographic writings, and viewing them as a group may aid memorization.

aʾlu (10.6)	LÚ.GIŠ.DA
abarakkatu	MUNUS.AGRIG
abarakku	LÚ.AGRIG
abarakkūtu (7-B)	MUNUS.AGRIG
abāru (ii) (10.7)	A.BÁR
ablu	ḪÁD.A
abnu (2-E)	NA_4
absinnu (10.7)	AB.SÍN
abu (1-C)	AD
abullu (2-E)	KÁ.GAL
adi (1-B)	EN
agû (i) (5-C)	AGA

agurru (4-C)	SIG$_4$.AL.ÙR.RA
aḫātu (8-C)	MUNUS.NIN
aḫātu (8-C)	NIN$_9$
aḫḫūtu (10.5)	ŠEŠ
aḫu (i) (2-D)	PAP
aḫu (i) (2-D)	ŠEŠ
akalu (8-A)	NINDA
akālu (5-G)	KÚ
akkullu (7-C)	NÍG.GUL
aladlammû (5-E)	^{d}ALAD.LAMMA
alāku (1-B)	DU
alandimmû	ALAM.DÍM
āliku (2-C)	DU
alluttu	MUL.AL.LUL
alpu (2-A)	GU$_4$
alpu (2-A)	GU$_4$.NÍTA
ālu (1-A)	URU
amāru (2-B)	IGI
amāru (2-B)	IGI.LÁ
ammatu (3-D)	KÙŠ
amtu	GÉME
amurdinnu	GIŠ.GEŠTIN.GÍR
amurru (10.14)	IM.MAR.TU
amūtu (10.7)	BÀ
andullu (8-F)	AN.DÙL
angubbû (10.5)	AN.GUB.BA
annaku (4-D)	AN.NA
annanna (10.7)	NENNI
annû (3-B)	NAM
annû (3-B)	ŠEŠ
annû (3-B)	Ú
annû (3-B)	Ù
antallû	AN.MI
anzû (8-E)	^{d}IM.DUGUD.MUŠEN
apkallu (6-D)	ABGAL
aplu (6-F)	IBILA
appāru (6-C)	GI.AMBAR
appatu (10.8)	KUŠ.PA
apsasû (5-B)	MUNUS.ÁB.ZA.ZA
apsasû (5-B)	ZA.ZA
apsû (6-C)	AB.ZU

apsû (6-C)	ZU.AB
apu (9-A)	GIŠ.GI
arāku (4-E)	GÍD
arāku (4-E)	GÍD.DA
arba'u (5-C)	LÍMMU
argamannu (6-C)	SÍG.ZA.GÌN.MI
argamannu (6-C)	SÍG.ZA.GÌN.SA$_5$
arḫu (ii)	GU$_4$.ÁB
arku (8-C)	GÍD.DA
arû	A.RÁ
asakku (i) (10.6)	ÁZAG
asakku (ii) (10.7)	AZAG
askuppu (5-D)	KUN$_4$
askuppu (5-D)	NA$_4$.KUN$_4$
aslu (ii) (5-G)	AS$_4$.LUM
asu (10.10)	AZ
asû	LÚ.A.ZU
ašāgu (10.9)	GIŠ.KIŠI$_{16}$
ašarēdu (4-D)	LÚ.SAG.KAL
ašarēdu (4-D)	SAG.KAL
ašarettu	SAG.KAL
ašgigû (10.9)	NA$_4$.AŠ.GÌ.GÌ
aškāpu	LÚ.AŠGAB
ašnugallu (4-B)	NA$_4$.GIŠ.NU.GAL
ašnugallu (4-B)	NA$_4$.GIŠ.NU$_{11}$.GAL
ašqulālu	Ú.LAL
ašru (1-C)	KI
aššatu (5-C)	DAM
ašūḫu (10.9)	GIŠ.Ù.SUḪ$_5$
atbaru (10.5)	NA$_4$.AD.BAR
atûtu	LÚ.Ì.DU$_8$
awātu (3-B)	INIM
awīl narkabti	LÚ.GIŠ.GIGIR
awīlu (5-D)	LÚ
ayyakku (10.8)	É.AN.NA
ayyalu (10.10)	DÀRA.MAŠ
ayyartu	NA$_4$.PA
bā'eru	LÚ.ŠU.KU$_6$
bābu (2-B)	KÁ
balāṭu (i) (2-E)	NAM.TI.LA
balāṭu (i) (2-E)	TI

balāṭu (i) (2-E)	TI.LA
balāṭu (i) (2-E)	TIN
baltu (10.10)	GIŠ.DÌḪ
balṭu (5-B)	TI
balṭu (5-B)	TI.LA
banduddû	GIŠ.BA.AN.DU_8.DU_8
bānû (2-D)	DÙ
barbaru	UR.BAR.RA
bārû (9-D)	LÚ.ḪAL
bārû (9-D)	MÁŠ.ŠU.GÍD.GÍD
barû (ii)	IGI.KÁR
bāštu (8-A)	TÉŠ
bāšû (3-D)	GÁL
bašû (i) (3-A)	GÁL
batultu (10.11)	MUNUS.KAL.TUR
batūlu (10.13)	LÚ.GURUŠ.TUR
bēl āli (5-A)	LÚ.EN.URU
bēl narkabti (8-A)	LÚ.EN GIŠ.GIGIR.MEŠ
bēl pīḫāti (3-C)	LÚ.EN.NAM
bēltu (2-B)	GAŠAN
bēltu (2-B)	NIN
bēlu (1-A)	EN
bēlu (1-A)	UMUN
berqu (9-A)	NIM.GÍR
bēru (iii) (4-C)	DANNA
bēru (iii) (4-C)	KASKAL.GÍD
billatu	DIDA
biltu (2-A)	GÚ.UN
biltu (2-A)	GUN
birku (7-G)	GÌŠ
birmu (4-C)	GÙN
birtu (i) (3-D)	URU.ḪAL.ṢU.MEŠ
bīt mayyāli	É.KI.NÁ
bītu (1-B)	É
būlu (7-E)	MÁŠ.ANŠE
buqlu (10.10)	$MUNU_4$
buqlu (10.10)	ŠE.BÙLUG.MEŠ
buqlu (10.10)	ŠE.$MUNU_4$
burāšu (5-D)	GIŠ.LI
burāšu (5-D)	GIŠ.ŠIM.LI
burāšu (5-D)	ŠIM.LI

bursaggû BUR.SAG.GÁ
būrtu (8-B) PÚ
būru (ii) (10.9) AMAR
būru (ii) (10.9) GU$_4$.AMAR
būšu (2-D) NÍG.ŠU
dabdû (2-E) BAD$_5$.BAD$_5$
dâku (2-B) GAZ
daltu (4-B) GIŠ.IG
dāmātu IM.SIG$_7$.SIG$_7$
damdāmu ANŠE.NUN
damqu (2-E) MUNUS.SIG$_5$
damqu (2-E) SIG
damqu (2-E) SIG$_5$
dāmu (5-A) MÚD
dāmu (5-A) ÚŠ
danānu (ii) (4-A) KALAG
dannatu (4-C) BAD$_4$
dannatu (4-C) KAL
dannatu (4-C) MUNUS.KALA
dannu (1-B) KAL
dannu (1-B) KALA
dannūtu (3-C) KAL
dayyānu (6-C) DI.KU$_5$
dekû (2-D) ZI
dīktu (3-B) GAZ
dikuggallu (10.12) DI.KU$_5$.GAL
dikuggallu (10.12) DI.KUD.GAL
dimtu (i) (8-H) URU.AN.ZA.GÀR
diqāru (5-D) ÚTUL
dišpu (8-H) LÀL
dumqu (5-E) SIG$_5$
dūru (i) (2-B) BÀD
dūru (i) (2-B) BÀD.KI
dušû (10.11) KUŠ.DUḪ.ŠI.A
ebūru (6-A) BURU$_{14}$
edēšu (2-C) GIBIL
egalturrû (9-A) É.GAL.TUR.RA
egerrû (10.9) INIM.GAR
ēkallu (1-B) É.GAL
ekēmu (3-C) KAR
ēkurru (3-E) É.KUR

elât šamê	AN.PA
elēnû (7-E)	AN.TA
eleppu (4-E)	GIŠ.MÁ
eli (1-B)	UGU
eliš (5-E)	AN.TA
elītu (10.8)	AN.TA
ellu (3-B)	KÙ
elû (iii) (2-C)	E_{11}
elû (ii)	AN.TA
elû (i) (5-A)	AN.TA
emūqu (3-B)	Á
emūqu (3-B)	Á.KAL
engisû	NA_4.EN.GI.SA_6
enšu (7-I)	SIG
enû (6-C)	BAL
eperu (5-C)	SAḪAR
epēšu (1-B)	DÙ
epinnu (10.10)	GIŠ.APIN
epinnu (10.10)	MUL.APIN
ēpišu (3-C)	DÙ
eqlu (4-D)	A.ŠÀ
erbe (2-D)	LÍMMU
erbû (8-H)	$BURU_5$
erbu (ii) (6-C)	ŠÚ
erēbu (2-A)	KU_4
erēnu (2-D)	EREN
ereqqu (10.10)	GIŠ.MAR.GÍD.DA
ereqqu (10.10)	MUL.MAR.GÍD.DA
erēšu (ii) (7-H)	KAM
ēribu (10.8)	LÚ.KU_4
erṣetu (2-C)	KI
eršaḫungû	ÉR.ŠÀ.ḪUN.GÁ
eršu (iv) (5-D)	GIŠ.NÁ
erû (i) (8-H)	TI_8.MUŠEN
eṣēdu (i) (10.6)	ŠE.KIN.TAR
eṣemtu (7-H)	GÌR.PAD.DA
eṣemtu (7-H)	GÌR.PAD.DU
ešēru (3-A)	SI.SÁ
ešmarû (8-C)	GU.AN.NA
eššēšu (10.8)	ÈŠ.ÈŠ
eššu (10.13)	GIBIL

etellu (7-H)	NIR.GÁL
etēqu (4-A)	DIB
eṭemmu (10.6)	GIDIM
eṭlu (4-C)	LÚ.GURUŠ
ezzu (4-D)	ḪUŠ
gabadibbu (3-C)	GABA.DIB
gabarû (9-D)	GABA.RI
gadamāḫu	GADA.MAḪ
gallû (9-B)	GAL$_5$.LÁ
gāmilu (10.13)	ŠU
gammalu (4-B)	ANŠE.A.AB.BA
gammalu (4-B)	ANŠE.GAM.MAL
gamru (10.5)	AL.TIL
gamru (10.5)	TIL
ganūnu (10.7)	GÁ.NUN
gaṣṣu	IM.BABBAR
gerru (2-B)	KASKAL
gidubbû	GI.DUB
girim ḫilibê (10.6)	NA$_4$.GI.RIM.ḪI.LI.BA
girim ḫilibê (10.6)	NA$_4$.GIRIM.ḪI.LI.BA.
girtablilu	GÍR.TAB.LÚ.U$_{18}$.LU
gīru (3-B)	^{d}GIŠ.BAR
gišḫurru (9-D)	GIŠ.ḪUR
gišimmaru (10.10)	GIŠ.GIŠIMMAR
gišimmaru (10.10)	GIŠ.NÍG.TUKU
gištappu (10.6)	GIŠ.GÌR.GUB
gugallu (7-G)	GÚ.GAL
guḫlu (9-A)	NA$_4$.ŠIM.BI.ZI.DA.
gumāḫu (10.14)	GU$_4$.MAḪ
gurrutu	U$_8$
gušūru (3-D)	GIŠ.GUŠUR
gušūru (3-D)	GIŠ.ÙR
ḫadîš (4-B)	ḪÚL
ḫalāqu (3-A)	ZÁḪ
ḫaluppu	GIŠ.ḪA.LU.ÚB
ḫammā'u (10.12)	NÍ.GI
ḫarrānu (3-C)	KASKAL
ḫašḫūru	GIŠ.ḪAŠḪUR
ḫašūru (10.9)	GIŠ.ḪA.ŠUR
ḫašūru (10.9)	GIŠ.ḪAŠḪUR
ḫaṭṭu (4-D)	GIŠ.GIDRU

ḫaṭṭu (4-D)	GIŠ.NÍG.GIDRU
ḫengallu (5-F)	ḪE.GÁL
ḫidiātu (6-A)	ḪÚL
ḫilēpu	GIŠ.KÌM
ḫilibû (10.6)	NA$_4$.GI.RIM.ḪI.LI.BA
ḫimētu (9-B)	Ì.NUN
ḫīpu (10.13)	GAZ
ḫittu (10.12)	GIŠ.GAN.DU$_7$
ḫulālu	NA$_4$.NÍR
ḫurāpu	UDU.NIM
ḫurāṣu (1-C)	KÙ.GI
ḫusāru	NA$_4$.KA.GI.NA.
ibilu (6-D)	ANŠE.A.AB.BA
Idiqlatiš	ÍD.ḪAL.ḪAL
idu (3-A)	Á
idugallu	Ì.DU$_8$.GAL
igāru (5-F)	É.GAR$_8$
igāru (5-F)	É.SIG$_4$
igigallu (10.5)	IGI.GÁL
igirû (10.14)	ÍGIRA.MUŠEN
igisû (6-D)	IGI.SÁ
ikkaru	LÚ.ENGAR
ikkibu (7-H)	NÍG.GIG
ikribu (3-B)	ŠÙD
ikû (10.5)	IKU
īku	E
illatu (5-F)	ILLAT
ilu (1-A)	DINGIR
imbaru (7-A)	MURU$_9$
imēru (i) (3-C)	ANŠE
imēru (i) (3-C)	ANŠE.NÍTA
imēru (ii) (5-F)	ANŠE
imitta	ZAG
immeru (3-C)	UDU
immeru (3-C)	UDU.NÍTA
imna (8-A)	ZAG
imnu (10.10)	ZAG
inbu (5-F)	GIŠ.GURUN
inbu (5-F)	GURUN
īnu (3-C)	IGI.II
inūma (2-D)	UD

irtu (4-E)	GABA
isḫunnatu	GIŠ.KIN.GEŠTIN
isinnu (6-E)	EZEN
isqu (7-G)	GIŠ.ŠUB.BA
isu	UZU.ME.ZÉ
iṣṣūru (4-C)	MUŠEN
iṣu (4-C)	GIŠ
išātu (2-D)	IZI
išdu (5-A)	SUḪUŠ
išdu (5-A)	ÚR
išid šamê	AN.ÚR
iškāru	ÉŠ.GÀR
iššiakku (2-A)	ÉNSI
iššiakku (2-A)	LÚ.ŠID
iššiakkūtu (10.14)	ŠID
ištānu (8-B)	IM.SI.SÁ
ištaru (4-C)	^{d}15
ištaru (4-C)	^{d}INANNA
ištaru (4-C)	^{d}IŠ.TAR
ištaru (4-C)	^{d}U.DAR
ištēn (3-E)	AŠ.ÀM
ištēnšerû	11
ištu (1-B)	TA
išû (i) (3-A)	TUK
išû (i) (3-A)	TUKU
itqūru	GIŠ.DÍLIM
itti (1-B)	KI
itti (1-B)	TA
ittu (i) (8-B)	Á
ittu (ii) (8-E)	GISKIM
ittu (ii) (8-E)	GIŠKIM
izuzzu (2-B)	GUB
kabātu	DUGUD
kabtu (2-C)	DUGUD
kakkabu (8-C)	MUL
kakku (1-C)	GIŠ.TUKUL
kalāma (5-A)	DÙ
kalāma (5-A)	DÙ.A.BI
kalbu (9-F)	UR.GI$_{7}$
kalītu	UZU.ÉLLAG
kallāpu (10.9)	LÚ.KAL.LAP

kalû (iii) (9-H)	LÚ.GALA
kalû (ii) (2-B)	DÙ
kamiššaru	GIŠ.ŠENNUR.BABBAR.RA
kamūnu (i)	Ú.GAMUN
kanaktu	GIŠ.ŠIM.GIG
kannu (10.10)	GIŠ.GAN
kanšu (4-A)	GÚR
kânu (2-A)	GIN
karābu (5-F)	ŠÙD
karānu (4-A)	GIŠ.GEŠTIN
karāšu (4-B)	KARAŠ
kāru (7-A)	KAR
kaspu (1-C)	KI.SAG
kaspu (1-C)	KÙ.BABBAR
kāsu	GÚ.ZI
kasû (ii)	GAZI.SAR
kāṣiru (9-H)	LÚ.KA.ṢIR
kašādu (1-B)	KUR
kašmaḫḫu	KAŠ.MAḪ
katāmu (5-F)	DUL
kawû (i)	AŠ.A.AN
kibru (2-B)	UB
kibtu	ŠE.GIG
kidinnu (8-E)	BAR
kidinnu (8-E)	UBARA
kigallu (9-F)	KI.GAL
kiḫullû	KI.ḪUL
kikiṭṭû	KÌD.KÌD
kīma (1-C)	GIM
kimaḫḫu (8-F)	KI.MAḪ
kimtu (6-A)	IM.RI.A
kīnu (3-D)	GI.NA
kīnu (3-D)	GIN
kinūnu (10.11)	KI.NE
kippatu (9-D)	GÚR
kirimaḫḫu (8-C)	GIŠ.KIRI$_6$.MAḪ
kirû (4-D)	GIŠ.KIRI$_6$
kisallu (6-A)	KISAL
kisalmāḫu (10.5)	KISAL.MAḪ
kiṣru (4-A)	KA.KEŠDA
kiṣru (4-A)	KI.ṢIR

kiṣru (4-A)	KIŠ
kišādu (4-A)	NA_4.GÚ
kišittu (3-A)	KUR
kiššatu (1-B)	KIŠ
kiššatu (1-B)	ŠÁR
kiššatu (1-B)	ŠÚ
kitû (4-E)	GADA
kitû (4-E)	GIŠ.GADA
kitû (4-E)	TÚG.GADA
kubšu	SAGŠU
kubšu	TÚG.SAGŠU
kūdanu (5-G)	ANŠE.GÌR.NUN.NA
kuduppānu	GIŠ.NU.ÚR.MA
kudurru (i) (6-E)	NÍG.DU
kukkallu	GUKKAL
kulīlu	KU_6.LÚ.U_{18}.LU
kunukku (8-E)	NA_4.KIŠIB
kupru (7-D)	ESIR
kupru (7-D)	ESIR.UD.A
kurkû (10.9)	KUR.GI
kurkû (10.9)	KUR.GI.MUŠEN
Kurnugi	KUR.NU.GI_4.A
kurru	GUR
kurunnu (8-F)	KURUN.NAM
kussû (2-A)	GIŠ.AŠ.TE
kussû (2-A)	GIŠ.AŠ.TI
kussû (2-A)	GIŠ.GU.ZA
kūṣu (9-F)	EN.TE.NA
kutīmu	LÚ.KÙ.DÍM
kuzbu (7-H)	ḪI.LI
lā (1-A)	NU
labīru (6-B)	LIBIR.RA
labīru (6-B)	SUMUN
labīru (6-B)	TIL
lamassu (4-E)	^{d}LAMMA
lamassu (4-E)	MUNUS.^{d}LAMMA
lē'u (10.7)	GIŠ.LE.U_5.UM
lē'u (10.7)	GIŠ.ZU
lē'û (5-D)	Á.GÁL
lemnu (4-C)	ḪUL
lemuttu (3-D)	MUNUS.ḪUL

leqû (3-C)	TI
lētu (10.14)	TE
libbu (1-B)	ŠÀ
libittu (4-B)	SIG_4
libittu (4-B)	SIG_5
liginnu	IM.GÍD.DA
lilissu	LI.LI.ÌZ.
līm (2-A)	LIM
līmâ	LIM-A.A
liptu (7-B)	TAG
līpu (5-F)	ŠÀ.BAL.BAL
lismu	$KAŠ_4$
lišānu (6-D)	EME
lītu (ii)	$ÁB.GU_4$
lītu (i) (3-D)	NÍG.È
lumnu (10.10)	ḪUL
lurmu (10.10)	GÁ.NA.MUŠEN
lurmu (10.10)	$GÁ.NU_{11}.MUŠEN$
mādu (2-D)	ḪI.A
magāru (5-G)	ŠE.GA
magulû (10.6)	GIŠ.MÁ.GU.LA
maḫāru (2-A)	IGI
maḫāṣu (2-E)	SÌG
māḫiru (5-E)	GABA.RI
maḫīru (8-F)	KI.LAM
makkūru (2-E)	NÍG.GA
malāḫu	$LÚ.MÁ.LAḪ_5$
malû (i) (5-G)	SA_5
manû (iv) (2-B)	MA.NA
manûtu	ŠID
manziat (10.5)	[d]TIR.AN.NA
maqlūtu (10.14)	GÍBIL
mār šipri (9-A)	LÚ.A KIN
mār šipri (9-A)	$LÚ.KIN.GI_4.A$
marru (ii) (10.8)	GIŠ.MAR
marṣiš (8-B)	GIG
marṣu (3-D)	GIG
marṣu (3-D)	TU.RA
mārtu (3-C)	DUMU.MUNUS
mārtu (3-C)	MUNUS.DUMU
māru (1-A)	A

māru (1-A)	DUMU
marû (i) (8-A)	NIGA
marû (i) (8-A)	ŠE
maruṣtu (9-B)	NÍG.GIG
masabbu (10.9)	MA.SÁ.AB
maṣṣartu (7-G)	EN.NUN
maṣṣaru (10.13)	EN.NUN
mašennu	LÚ.AGRIG
maškanu (6-E)	MAŠ.KÁN
mašku (4-D)	KUŠ
mašmaššu	MAŠ.MAŠ
māšu (10.14)	MAŠ.TAB.BA
mātu (1-A)	KALAM
mātu (1-A)	KUR
maṭû	LAL
mayyālu (9-F)	KI.NÁ
mazzāzu (5-F)	KI.GUB
meʾatu (1-C)	ME
meḫretu (4-B)	GABA
meḫretu (4-B)	IGI
meḫru (i) (10.11)	GABA.RI
melemmu (4-A)	ME.LÁM
mešēnu	KUŠ.DA.E.SIR
migru (4-A)	ŠE.GA
miḫiṣtu	GÙ.SUM
milku (6-B)	GALGA
mīlu (4-C)	A.KAL
mīlu (4-C)	ILLU
mīs pî (10.6)	KA.LUḪ.Ù.DA
mīs pî (10.6)	KA.LUḪ.UD.DA
mitgāru (10.13)	ŠE.GA
mītu	ÚŠ
miṭṭu (10.6)	GIŠ.KU.AN
miṭṭu (10.6)	GIŠ.TUKUL.DINGIR
mû (2-D)	A
muḫḫu (2-C)	UGU
mukabbû	LÚ.TÚG.KAL
mukillu (7-D)	LÚ.DAB
munawwiru (10.14)	ZÁLAG
mūraku (10.8)	GÍD
mūraku (10.8)	GÍD.DA

murru	ŠIM.SES
murṣu (10.12)	GIG
musukkannu (3-E)	GIŠ.MÁ.KAN.NA
musukkannu (3-E)	GIŠ.MES.MÁ.KAN
mušarû (2-D)	MU.SAR
mūšaru (10.7)	MU.SAR
mūšaru (10.7)	SAR
mušḫuššu	MUŠ.ḪUŠ
muškēnu	MAŠ.EN.GAG
mušlalaḫḫu	LÚ.MUŠ.LAḪ$_4$
muššāru (10.11)	NA$_4$.MUŠ.GÍR
mūšu (5-B)	GE$_6$
mūšu (5-B)	GI$_6$
mūtānu (10.10)	NAM.ÚŠ.MEŠ
mūtānu (10.10)	ÚŠ.MEŠ
mutḫummu (10.6)	NÍG.SA.SA
mūtu (7-E)	ÚŠ
muṭibbu (i) (10.6)	DÙG
nabalkutu (ii) (3-B)	BAL
nabalkutu (i)	BAL
nadānu (ii) (3-A)	SUM
nadnu (10.6)	SUM.MU
nādu (i) (10.9)	KUŠ.ÙMMU
nadû (i) (5-B)	ŠUB
nadû (iii) (2-B)	ŠUB
nagāru (10.5)	LÚ.NAGAR
nagbu (5-B)	IDIM
nāgiru (7-I)	LÚ.NIGIR
nāgiru (7-I)	LÚ.NIMGIR
naḫlaptu	TÚG.GÚ.È
nakāru (3-A)	KÚR
nakāsu (3-A)	KUD
nakru (ii) (2-A)	LÚ.KÚR
nakru (i) (6-F)	KÚR
nalbanu (10.13)	GIŠ.Ù.SUB
nalbattu (10.5)	GIŠ.Ù.ŠUB
nannāru (8-G)	^{d}ŠEŠ.KI
napāḫu (9-A)	KUR
napḫaru (3-A)	NIGIN
napḫaru (3-A)	PAP
napḫaru (3-A)	ŠU.NIGIN

napḫaru (3-A)	ŠU.NÍGIN
napištu (2-B)	ZI
nappāḫu	LÚ.SIMUG
nāqidūtu	NA.GADA
naqû (2-E)	BAL
narāmu (4-B)	ÁGA
nargallu	LÚ.NAR.GAL
narkabtu (2-A)	GIŠ.GIGIR
narpasu	GIŠ.MAR.ŠE.RA.AḪ
nārtu (i) (9-G)	ÍD
nārtu (ii) (7-G)	MUNUS.NAR
narû (2-D)	NA$_4$.NA.RÚ
narû (2-D)	NA$_4$.NA.RÚ.A
nāru (ii) (6-B)	LÚ.NAR
nāru (i) (3-D)	ÍD
nasāḫu (3-C)	ZI
nasḫuru	NIGIN
naṣāru (4-B)	PAP
nāṣiru (4-E)	PAP
našû (ii) (2-E)	ÍL
nawāru (4-A)	ZÁLAG
nazuzzu	GUB
neʾrāru (10.7)	ERIM.TÁḪ
nēr (7-D)	GÉŠ.U
nêšakku (9-I)	LÚ.NU.ÈŠ
nēšu (6-B)	UR.MAḪ
nignakku (10.7)	NÍG.NA
nikkassu	NÍG.KA$_9$
niksu (6-C)	KUD
nindabû (8-D)	NIDBA
nindanu (7-G)	NINDA
nīqu (2-E)	SISKUR
nīqu (2-E)	SÍSKUR
nīqu (2-E)	UDU.SISKUR
nīqu (2-E)	UDU.SÍSKUR
nīru (2-B)	GIŠ.DUN$_4$
nīru (2-B)	GIŠ.GIŠ
nīru (2-B)	GIŠ.ŠUDUN
nīšu (ii) (7-H)	MU
nišu (1-B)	UN
nuḫatimmu	LÚ.MUḪALDIM

nuḫšu (5-F)	ḪÉ.NUN
nukaribbu (10.6)	LÚ.NU.GIŠ.KIRI$_6$
nukurtu (10.5)	MUNUS.KÚR
nūnu (6-E)	KU$_6$
nurmû	GIŠ.NU.ÚR.MA
nūru (6-F)	ZÁLAG
pagru (4-B)	ADDA
pagru (4-B)	LÚ.ÀD
palāsu (4-B)	IGI.BAR
palgu (10.9)	PA$_5$
palû (2-A)	BALA
pāna (5-E)	IGI
pānu (1-C)	IGI
papāḫu (7-I)	É.PA.PAḪ
pappardaliu (7-C)	NA$_4$.BABBAR.DILI
papparmīnu (10.6)	NA$_4$.BABBAR.MIN$_5$
parakku (3-C)	BÁRA
paramāḫu (9-I)	BÁRA.MAḪ
parāsu (5-A)	KUD
pārisu (9-G)	KUD
parkullu	BUR.GUL
parsiktu	PI
parṣu (4-E)	GARZA
parû (i) (3-D)	ANŠE.KUNGA
parzillu (3-B)	AN.BAR
paspasu (10.7)	UZ.TUR.MUŠEN
pašāru (10.10)	BÚR
pašāšu (4-A)	ŠÉŠ
pašqu (5-F)	ḪUL
paššuru (7-A)	GIŠ.BANŠUR
patru (5-D)	GÍR
patru (5-D)	GÍR.AN.BAR
patru (5-D)	GIŠ.GÍR
paṭīru	GI.DU$_8$
pāṭu (2-D)	ZAG
pelû	NUNUZ
pendû (9-E)	NA$_4$.^{d}ŠE.TIR
per'u (6-A)	NUNUZ
peṣû (4-E)	BABBAR
peṣû (4-E)	KÙ
petû (i) (7-A)	BAD

pīḫātu (2-C)	LÚ.EN.NAM
pīḫātu (2-C)	LÚ.NAM
pilaqqu	GIŠ.BAL
piriggallu (10.14)	PIRIG.GAL
pirištu (7-E)	AD.ḪAL
pīru (3-D)	AM.SI
pišannu	PISAN
pīt bābi (10.6)	ITI.BAD.KÁ
pīt pî (10.5)	KA.DU$_8$.Ù.DA
pīt pî (10.5)	KA.DU$_8$.UD.DA
pitnu (10.8)	GIŠ.NA$_5$
pitnu (10.8)	NA$_5$
pû (ii)	KA
puḫādu	UDU.SILA$_4$
puḫru (5-A)	UKKIN
pulukku (10.8)	BULUG
pūru (i)	BUR
purussû (5-D)	EŠ.BAR
pušqu (10.10)	PAP.ḪAL
pūtu (3-E)	SAG
pūtu (3-E)	SAG.KI
qabaltu (7-B)	MURUB$_4$
qablû (10.10)	MURUB$_4$
qablu (ii) (3-D)	MURUB$_4$
qablu (i) (2-D)	MURUB$_4$
qabû (2-B)	DU$_{11}$.GA
qabû (2-B)	DUG$_4$.GA
qalû (ii) (10.14)	GÍBIL
qanû (5-D)	GI
qanû (5-D)	GIŠ.GI
qaqqadu (3-A)	SAG.DU
qarnu (9-E)	SI
qarrādu (6-F)	UR.SAG
qaštu (3-C)	GIŠ.PAN
qaštu (3-C)	MUL.PAN
qātu (1-B)	ŠU
qēmu	ZÌ.DA
qiāšu (4-A)	BA
qiāšu (4-A)	NÍG.BA
qiāšu (4-A)	SUM
qilûtu (6-F)	GÍBIL

qīpu (5-G)	LÚ.TIL.GÍD
qištu (6-F)	GIŠ.TIR
qīštu (7-E)	NÍG.BA
qû (ii)	SÌLA
qû (i) (9-E)	GU
qurādu (3-E)	UR.SAG
qurqurru	TIBIRA
rā'imu (5-B)	ÁGA
rab kāri	LÚ.GAL.KAR
rab ṭupšarri	LÚ.GAL.GI.BÙR
rab-šāqê (10.8)	LÚ.GAL.BI.LUL
rābiṣu (10.6)	MAŠKIM
rābiṣu (10.6)	MÁŠKIM
rabû (i) (1-A)	GAL
rabû (i) (1-A)	LÚ.GAL
rakābu (6-B)	U_5
rakbû (6-B)	LÚ.RA.GABA
ramānu (3-C)	NÍ
râmu (ii) (5-E)	ÁG
râmu (ii) (5-E)	ÁGA
rapšu (2-C)	DAGAL
raqqu (ii)	BAL.GI.KU_6
rašû (3-D)	TUK
rē'û (4-A)	LÚ.SIPA
rē'û (4-A)	RE.É.UM
rebītu (6-F)	SILA.DAGAL.LA
rebû (8-A)	4
rēdû (10.8)	LÚ.UKU.UŠ
rēdû (10.8)	LÚ.UŠ
rēmēnû (7-H)	RÉM
rēmu (4-E)	$AGARIN_4$
rēmu (4-E)	ARḪUŠ
rēṣūtu (4-B)	Á.TAḪ
rēštu (6-E)	SAG
rēštû (6-A)	SAG
rēšu (2-A)	SAG
riḫṣu (10.14)	GÌR.BAL
rīmu (5-C)	AM
rīmu (5-C)	GU_4.AM
rīqu (5-A)	ŠIM
rittu (5-C)	KIŠIB

rubātu	ÉGI
rubû (2-A)	LÚ.GAL
rubû (2-A)	NUN
rupšu (6-E)	DAGAL
rūqu (2-C)	SÙ
ruššû (6-A)	ḪUŠ
ruššû (6-A)	ḪUŠ.A
rūštu (10.13)	Ì.SAG
saḫaršubbû	SAḪAR.ŠUB.BA
saḫliu (10.12)	Ú.ZAG.ḪI.LI
saḫliu (10.12)	Ú.ZAG.ḪI.LI.SAR
samānēšret (10.5)	18
samānû (10.14)	8
sammû (10.7)	GIŠ.ZÀ.MÍ
sāmtu (10.13)	NA_4.GUG
sāmu (10.9)	SA_5
sangilimud (10.5)	NA_4.SAG.GIL.MUD
santakku	$SANTAK_4$
sapḫu (10.11)	BIR
sattukku (5-B)	SÁ.DUG_4
sebîšu	7
sebû (10.10)	7
sekret ēkalli (8-B)	MUNUS.ERIM.É.GAL
sekretu (6-A)	MUNUS.ERIM
serremtu	MUNUS.ANŠE.EDIN.NA
serrēmu (10.13)	ANŠE.EDIN.NA
siḫirtu (2-C)	NIGIN
sikkatu (5-A)	GAG
sikkūru	SAG.KUL
sinništu (5-B)	MUNUS
siparru (2-D)	ŠU.KA.AN
siparru (2-D)	ZABAR
sīrāšû (10.7)	LÚ.LÚNGA
sissiktu	TÚG.SÍG
sisû (2-A)	ANŠE.KUR
sisû (2-A)	ANŠE.KUR.RA
suādu	ŠIM.EN.DI
suḫurmāšu	SUḪUR.MÁŠ.KU_6
sukannīnu	TU.KUR_4.MUŠEN
sukkalmaḫḫu	LÚ.SUKKAL.MAḪ
suluppu (9-C)	ZÚ.LUM.MA

summatu (10.5)	TU.MUŠEN
sūqu (7-A)	SILA
surdû	SÚR.DÙ.MUŠEN
sūtu	BÁN
ṣabātu (1-C)	DAB
ṣabātu (1-C)	DIB
ṣabītu (9-C)	MAŠ.DÀ
ṣābu (2-A)	ERIM
ṣābu (2-A)	LÚ.ERIM
ṣalmāt-qaqqadi	SAG.GE_6.GA.A
ṣalmu (i) (6-B)	GE_6
ṣalmu (ii) (2-C)	ALAM
ṣalmu (ii) (2-C)	NU
ṣeḫru (ii) (7-D)	TUR
ṣeḫru (i) (3-A)	TUR
ṣēnu (iii) (2-C)	U_8
ṣēnu (iii) (2-C)	US_5.UDU
ṣerru (i) (10.14)	MUŠ
ṣēru (1-C)	EDIN
ṣētu	UD.DA
ṣibtu (ii) (10.5)	MÁŠ
ṣibtu (i) (10.11)	MÁŠ
ṣillu (9-E)	GIŠ.MI
ṣimittu (5-A)	GIŠ.LAL
ṣīru (i) (2-A)	MAḪ
ṣīru (ii) (7-B)	LÚ.EDIN
ṣīru (ii) (7-B)	LÚ.MAḪ
ṣītu (3-C)	È
ṣubātu (10.13)	TÚG
ṣuḫāru	LÚ.TUR
ṣulūlu (6-C)	AN.DÙL
ṣumlalû	GIŠ.ŠIM.GAM.MA
ṣurru (ii) (8-E)	NA_4.ZÚ
ša (i) (1-A)	LÚ
ša ēkalli (6-A)	MUNUS.É.GAL
ša ēkalli (6-A)	MUNUS.KUR
ša ēkalli (6-A)	MUNUS.ŠÀ.É.GAL
ša rēši	LÚ.SAG
šabrû (i)	ŠAPRA
šaddidu	LÚ.GÍD.DA
šadû (ii) (9-E)	IM.KUR.RA

šadû (i) (1-B)	KUR
šagigurrû (10.10)	ŠÀ.GI.GURU$_6$
šagigurrû (10.10)	ŠÀ.GI.GURU$_6$.A
šaḫû (7-H)	ŠAḪ
šakānu (1-B)	GÁ
šakānu (1-B)	GAR
šakin māti (6-A)	LÚ.GAR.KUR
šākinu (6-C)	GAR
šakkanakku (2-E)	GÌR.ARAD
šakkanakku (2-E)	LÚ.GÌR.NITA
šaknu (ii) (2-B)	LÚ.GAR
šaknu (i) (4-C)	GAR
šalamtu (6-E)	ADDA
šalāmu (ii) (3-E)	SILIM
šalāmu (i) (10.6)	SILIM
šalāšī- (9-I)	3
šalaššerû	13
šalḫû (6-B)	BÀD.ŠUL.ḪI
šalḫû (6-B)	BÀD.ŠUL.ḪU
šalšu (8-A)	3
šamallû	LÚ.ŠÁMAN.LÁ
šaman pūri	Ì.BUR
šamaškillu	Ú.SUM.SIKIL.SAR
šamaššammū	ŠE.GIŠ.Ì
šammu (9-E)	Ú
šamnu (3-B)	Ì
šamnu (3-B)	Ì.GIŠ
šamšu (3-A)	ᵈUTU
šamû (2-B)	AN
šanānu (4-B)	SÁ
šandabakku (9-A)	LÚ.GÚ.EN.NA
šangû (7-D)	É.BAR
šangû (7-D)	LÚ.SANGA
šanîš (10.10)	KI.MIN
šanû (ii) (5-A)	LÚ.2
šanû (ii) (5-A)	MAN
šanû (i) (5-G)	LÚ.2
šanûti- (9-A)	2
šaplītu	KI.TA
šaplû (4-D)	KI.TA
šaplu (ii) (7-B)	KI.TA

šappu	DUG.ŠAB
šaptu (5-C)	NUNDUM
šāqû	BI.LUL
šaqû (iii) (9-C)	NAG
šaqû (i) (4-E)	LAL
šār (6-F)	ŠÁR
šār (6-F)	$ŠAR_5$
šarāku (3-E)	A.MU.RU
šarāpu (3-A)	GÍBIL
šārī erbetti	IM.LÍMMU.BA
šarku	LUGUD
šarru (1-A)	LUGAL
šarru (1-A)	MAN
šāru (i) (6-D)	IM
šassūru (10.8)	ŠÀ.TÙR
šaššūgu	GIŠ.SÙḪ.NA
šatammu (10.7)	LÚ.ŠÀ.TAM
šattišamma (4-B)	MU.AN.NA
šattišamma (4-B)	MU.DIŠ.KÁM
šattu (3-B)	AD.ME.KÁR
šattu (3-B)	MU
šaṭru (3-C)	AB.SAR
šaṭru (3-C)	SAR
šawiru (7-D)	ḪAR
še'u (10.7)	ŠE.PAD.LIM
še'u (10.7)	ŠE.UM
šēdu (7-D)	^{d}ALAD
šēlebu	KA_5.A
šeleppû	NÍG.BÚN.NA.KU_6
šemû (2-A)	ŠE.GA
šēnu	KUŠ.E.SÍR
šēpu (1-C)	GÌR
šeriktu (6-E)	RU
šešgallūtu	LÚ.ŠEŠ.GAL
šeššu (i) (10.14)	6
šī (5-E)	BI
šibirru (8-D)	GIŠ.ŠIBIR
šību (10.8)	LÚ.AB.BA
šību (10.8)	LÚ.ŠU.GI
šiddu (3-C)	ÚS.SA.DU
šiddu (3-C)	UŠ

šigaru (5-F)	SI.GAR
šikaru (7-G)	KAŠ
šikaru (7-G)	KAŠ.SAG
šikkû (10.8)	^{d}NIN.KILIM
šiltāḫu (8-A)	GIŠ.GAG.U$_4$.TAG.GA
šimiššalû	GIŠ.ŠIM.ŠAL
šīmtu (3-B)	NAM
šīmtu (3-B)	^{d}NAM
šīmu	ŠÁM
šinipu	ŠANABI
šinni pīri (5-F)	ZÚ AM.SI
šinni ṣabīti (10.6)	NA$_4$.ZÚ.MAŠ.DÀ
šinnu (3-D)	NA$_4$.ZÚ
šinnu (3-D)	ZÚ
šinšariu	12
šīpātu (8-B)	SÍG
šīpātu (8-B)	SÍK
šipru (2-A)	KIN
šiqlu (7-A)	GÍN
šīru (4-E)	UZU
šiteʾû	BU.BU.LU
šitimgallu (10.11)	LÚ.ŠITIM.GAL
šiṭru (2-D)	SAR
šizbu	GA
šuʾillakku	ŠU.ÍL.KÁM
šuāti (2-A)	MU
šuāti (2-A)	UR$_5$
šubtu (2-B)	KI.TUŠ
šukkallu (7-D)	LÚ.SUKKAL
šulmu (3-B)	SILIM
šumēla (7-E)	2.30
šumēla (7-E)	GÙB
šumēlu (10.13)	2.30
šumēlu (10.13)	GÙB
Šumeru	EME.GI$_7$
šumma (10.8)	DIŠ
šumu (1-B)	MU
šūmū	Ú.SUM.SAR
šupālû (10.8)	KI.TA
šuqultu (6-C)	KI.LÁ
šurmēnu (3-E)	GIŠ.ŠUR.MÌN

šūši (4-E)	60
šūši (4-E)	UŠ
šūt rēši (2-C)	LÚ.SAG
šuttu (6-D)	MÁŠ.GE_6
šuttu (6-D)	MÁŠ.GI_6
šūtu (ii) (8-E)	IM.U_{18}.LU
tabālu (7-I)	TÙM
tāḫāzu (2-A)	MÈ
takiltu (6-F)	SÍG.ZA.GÌN.MI
takkassu (10.11)	NA_4.DAG.GAZ
tāmartu (3-D)	IGI.DU_8.A
tāmartu (3-D)	IGI.LAL
tamkāru	LÚ.DAM.GÀR
tarāṣu (4-B)	LAL
tarbaṣu (10.13)	TÙR
tarkullu	TÁR.KÍL
tarlugallu (10.9)	DAR.LUGAL.MUŠEN
tarṣu (4-D)	LAL
târu (1-C)	GUR
taskarinnu (3-E)	GIŠ.TÚG
tašlīšu (10.10)	LÚ.3.U_5
tebû (4-B)	ZI
teleʾû	ZÍB
têrtu (8-G)	UZU.UR_5.ÚŠ
tiāmtu (1-C)	A.AB.BA
tiāmtu (1-C)	AB
tibnu (8-D)	GIŠ.IN.NU
tibnu (8-D)	ŠE.IN.NU
tību (4-C)	ZI
tillatu (10.10)	ILLAT
tīlu (3-E)	DU_6
tīlu (3-E)	DUL
tinūru	NINDU
tīru (10.14)	LÚ.TIRUM
tišû	9
tittu	GIŠ.PÈŠ
tuqumtu (5-C)	GIŠ.LÁ
tuqumtu (5-C)	GIŠ.LAL
turāḫu (10.6)	DÀRA
turminabandû (6-C)	NA_4.DÚR.MI.NA.BÀN.DA
turminû (10.5)	NA_4.DÚR.MI.NA

ṭabtu (7-G)	MUN
ṭābtu (5-E)	DÙG.GA
ṭābtu (5-E)	MUN
ṭābu (3-C)	DUG
ṭābu (3-C)	DÙG.GA
ṭebû (9-A)	SÙ
ṭeḫû (8-B)	TE
ṭēḫu (7-I)	SUḪUR
ṭēmu (3-D)	SAG.DIN
ṭēmu (3-D)	UMUŠ
ṭīdu (10.14)	IM
ṭūbu (5-F)	DÙG
ṭūbu (5-F)	DÙG.GA
ṭuppu (7-F)	DUB
ṭuppu (7-F)	DUB.BI
ṭupšarru (7-H)	A.ZU
ṭupšarru (7-H)	LÚ.A.BA
ṭupšarru (7-H)	LÚ.DUB.SAR
û (6-A)	ŠE
û (6-A)	ŠE
û (6-A)	ŠE.AM
û (6-A)	ŠE.IM
û (6-A)	ŠE.PAD
ubānu (5-D)	ŠU.SI
ugallu	U_4.GAL
ugāru (7-B)	A.GÀR
uḫḫuzu (10.14)	GAR.RA
uḫulgallu	U_4.ḪUL.GÁL.E
ūm eššēši	UD.ÈŠ.ÈŠ
ummānu (1-C)	ERIM
ummānu (1-C)	ḪI.A
ummiānu (5-F)	UM.ME.A
ummu (i) (5-E)	AMA
ummu (i) (5-E)	MUNUS.AMA
ūmu (i) (1-B)	UD
ūmu (ii) (10.7)	UD
uqnû (5-B)	NA_4.ZA.GÌN
uqnû (5-B)	SÍG.ZA.GÌN
uqnû (5-B)	ZA.GÌN
urḫu (4-D)	ITI
uridimmu	UR.IDIM

urigallu (9-G)	^{d}ÙRI.GAL
urītu (10.5)	MUNUS.ANŠE.KUR.RA
urmaḫḫu (6-D)	UR.MAḪ
urpatu (9-E)	DUNGU
uršānu (7-I)	DI.KUD
ūru	ÙR
uskāru	U$_4$.SAKAR
ūsu (ii)	MUŠEN.UZ
ūsu (ii)	UZ.MUŠEN
ūṣu (9-C)	GIŠ.KAK.TI
uṣultu	GÍR.TUR
uṣurtu (9-A)	GIŠ.ḪUR
ušparu (10.7)	GIŠ.UŠ.BAR
ušparu (10.7)	GIŠ.UŠBAR$_5$
uššu (2-C)	SUḪ
uššu (2-C)	UŠ$_8$
ušû (4-A)	GIŠ.ESI
ušumgallu (8-A)	BÚR.GAL
ušumgallu (8-A)	UŠUMGAL
ušummu	PÉŠ.GIŠ.GI
utullu (9-E)	UTUL
utūnu (10.14)	UDUN
uṭṭatu (10.14)	ŠE
uṭṭatu (10.14)	ŠE.BAR
uṭṭatu (10.14)	ŠE.PAD
uznu (4-D)	GEŠTU
waklu (7-H)	UGULA
wardatu (10.5)	KI.SIKIL
wardu (3-D)	ÌR
wardu (3-D)	LÚ.ARAD
warḫu (4-B)	ITI
warka (8-D)	EGIR
warki (3-B)	EGIR
warkītu (4-D)	EGIR
warkû (2-E)	EGIR
warqu	SIG$_7$
warqu	Ú.SAR
wāšipu (10.10)	LÚ.KA.PIRIG
wāšipu (10.10)	LÚ.KA.PÌRIG
wāšipu (10.10)	LÚ.MAŠ.MAŠ
werû (2-D)	URUDU

zagiddurû	NA_4.ZA.GÌN.$DURU_5$
zakāru (3-E)	MU
zaqāpu (4-C)	GIŠ.GUB
zarû (10.6)	MAR
zēru (ii) (2-C)	NUMUN
zēru (ii) (2-C)	ŠE.NUMUN
zibbatu	KUN
zikaru (3-E)	NITA
zikaru (3-E)	NÍTA
zikru (2-C)	MU
ziqqurratu (5-G)	U_6.NIR
zubbu	NIM
zumru (8-E)	SU
zunnu (6-E)	ŠÈG
zuqiqīpu (10.9)	GÍR.TAB

APPENDIX F: LIST OF DIVINE NAMES

This appendix consists of two parts. The first is a list of the gods that occur in Assyrian royal inscriptions, along with a report of how frequently each god occurs in the corpus. The second part of this appendix is an alphabetized list of the logographic writings of divine names that appear in the corpus.

Gods Appearing in Assyrian Royal Inscriptions

God	Occurrences
Abirillu	3
Abšušu	2
Abtagigi	2
Adad	418
Agušaya	1
Amman-kasi-MAŠ	2
Amurriqanu	4
Amurru	7
Antu	8
Anu	176
Anu-rabu	8
Anunitu	6
Anunnaku	54
Anzu	4
Armada	1
Asalluhi	6
Asari (Marduk)	4
Aššur	2,723
Aššur-Enlil	2
Atar-quruma	3
Atar-samayin	11
Aya	18
Ayapagsina	2
Bagbartu	10
Bahar	1
Be'al-SI.SI	1
Bel	226
Bel-ibriya	1
Bel-labira	1
Bel-ṣarbi	2
Bel-šarri	1
Belet-Arba-il	3
Belet-Babili	11
Belet-balaṭi	2
Belet-ekallim	2
Belet-ili	33
Belet-Ninua	4
Belet-parṣi	15
Belet-ša-reši	1
Belet-ša-Uruk	2

Name	Count
Belet-šame	1
Beltiya	23
Ber	3
Bilala	2
Burruqu	1
Dagan	31
Damkina	4
Daragal	1
Daya	3
Dibar	1
Dilbat	4
Dinitu	9
Dumuzi	1
Dunga	4
Duranki	1
Ea	130
Ea-šarru	2
Egalkiba	3
En'e'imdu	2
Enbilulu	2
Enlil	499
Ennugi	1
Enpi	2
Ereškigal	3
Erra	20
Erua (Ṣarpanitu)	4
Ešerete	1
Girru	4
Gubaba	1
Gula	19
Gušea	1
Haldi	24
Hallasua	1
Hanibiya	1
Haya	8
Humhumiya	1
Igigi	70
Inanna	3
Innini	1
Inšušinak	4
Irnina	2
Išhara	1
Ištar	841
Ištar-kakkabi	1
Ištar-kudnittu	2
Ištar-šarrum	1
Ištaran	1
Išum	5
Itur-Mer	2
Kaka	3
Kalkal	3
Karhuha	1
Karsa	2
Kaššitu	1
Kidmuri	4
Kidudu	2
Kindakarbu	2
Kingu	1
Kippat-mati	1
Kirsamas	2
Kubaba	1
Kubu	1
Kulla	22
Kurunitum	1
Kurunnam	1
Kusibanda	8
Kusu	9
Kuturšar	2
Kutušar	1
Lagamaru	3
Lamma-RA.BI	9
Laṣ	8
Lugal-dingirra	1
Lugaldimmeranki	1
Lumha	3
Makurru	3
Mamu	3
Mandanu	8
Mar-biti	4
Mar-biti-ša-birit-nari	1
Mar-biti-ša-pan-biti	1
Marduk	382

Mina-ikul-beli	1	Nusku	140
Mullissu	155	Palil	4
Mušda	1	Panintimri	2
Muzibsa	1	Partikira	2
Nabirtu	2	Piriggal	1
Nabsa	2	Piṭuh-idugul	1
Nabu	367	Ragiba	2
Namraṣit	6	Ruldawu	3
Nanaya	43	Sadarnunna	3
Nanna	11	Sakkud	2
Nannaru	26	Salmanu	3
Naru	4	Samnuha	7
Ner-e-tagmil	1	Sapag	2
Nergal	221	Sebetti	23
Ninagal	20	Sigga	1
Ninbaragesi	1	Silagara	2
Nindagud	1	Sin	435
Ninegal	2	Sumuqan	3
Ningal	61	Sun-GAM-sara	2
Ningirima	3	Sutiti	2
Ningišzida	1	Ṣarpanitu	74
Ninildu	1	Šala	9
Ninimma	1	Šamaš	579
Ninkasik	1	Šargaz	2
Ninkura	12	Šarrat-Deri	3
Ninlil	3	Šarrat-Kidmuri	36
Ninmah	4	Šarrat-Ninua	2
Ninmena	4	Šarrat-niphi	10
Ninmenanna	1	Šarrat-Nippur	4
Ninsaggirgi	1	Šarru-matim	1
Ninšiku	14	Šarur	6
Ninuaittu	4	Šatru	3
Ninurta	217	Šauška	1
Ninzadim	4	Šazu	2
Nirah	1	Šeru	1
Nisaba	28	Šerua	15
Nudimmud	15	Šikaggu	1
Nuhaya	3	Šimaliya	1
Nunnamnir	13	Šudanu	2
Nunurra	1	Šukanaya	1
Nuru	4	Šulpaea	1

Šumudu	2	Ulay	1
Šuqamuna	1	Uraš	8
Šuziana	1	Urkayitu	6
Tašmetu	58	Uṣur-amassa	9
Tiamat	7	Utulu	6
Tišpak	1	Zababa	4
Uduran	2		

Logographic Writings of Divine Names

ᵈ7.BI	Sebetti
10	Adad
ᵈ10	Adad
ᵈ10-te	Ešerete
ᵈ15	Ištar
ᵈ30	Sin
ᵈ50	Enlil
ᵈ60	Anu
ᵈA.EDIN	Erua (Ṣarpanitu)
ᵈA.EDIN	Šerua
ᵈA.NUN.NA	Anunnaku
ᵈAB	Enlil
ᵈAG	Nabu
ᵈAMAR.UTU	Marduk
AN	Anu
ᵈAN	Anu
AN.GAL	Anu-rabu
ᵈAN.MAR.TU	Amurru
AN.ŠÁR	Aššur
AŠ	Aššur
ᵈAŠ.IM$_5$.BABBAR	Namraṣit
BAD	Enlil
ᵈBAD	Enlil
ᵈDÀR.GAL	Daragal
ᵈDI.KU$_5$	Mandanu
ᵈDÍM	Mušda
DINGIR.MAḪ	Belet-ili
ᵈDIŠ	Ea
ᵈDUMU.É	Mar-biti
ᵈEN	Bel

EN	Bel
^{d}EN.LIBIR.RA	Bel-labira
^{d}EN.LÍL	Enlil
^{d}EN.LÍL.LÁ	Enlil
^{d}EN.LÍL.LÁ.KE$_{4}$	Enlil
^{d}EN.LÍL.LA$_{5}$	Enlil
^{d}EN.ZU	Sin
^{d}EN-LUGAL	Bel-šarri
^{d}GAŠAN	Beltiya
^{d}GAŠAN-GARZA	Belet-parṣi
^{d}GAŠAN-KUR	Šarrat-niphi
^{d}GAŠAN-MU	Beltiya
^{d}GÉŠ.U	Anunnaku
^{d}GIBIL$_{6}$	Girru
^{d}GIŠ.BAR	Girru
^{d}GÚR-KUR	Kippat-mati
^{d}ÍD	Naru
^{d}IDIM	Ea
^{d}IGI.DU	Nergal
^{d}IGI.DU	Palil
^{d}IGI.SIG$_{7}$.SIG$_{7}$	Amurriqanu
^{d}IMIN.BI	Sebetti
^{d}INANNA	Ištar
^{d}INANNA.LUGAL	Ištar-šarrum
^{d}INANNA.MUL.MEŠ	Ištar-kakkabi
^{d}IŠKUR	Adad
^{d}IZI.GAR	Nuru
^{d}KA.DI	Ištaran
^{d}LAMMA-RA.BI	Lamma-RA.BI
^{d}LUGAL-GIŠ.ASAL	Bel-ṣarbi
^{d}MÁ.GUR$_{8}$	Makurru
^{d}MAR.TU	Amurru
^{d}MAŠ	Ninurta
^{d}MAŠ.MAŠ	Nergal
^{d}MAŠ.MAŠ	Ninurta
^{d}ME.ME	Gula
^{d}MES	Marduk
^{d}MUATI	Nabu
^{d}MUŠ	Nirah
^{d}MÙŠ.EREN	Inšušinak
^{d}MÙŠ.ŠÉŠ	Inšušinak

dNÈ.ERI$_{11}$.GAL	Nergal
dNIN.GAL	Ningal
dNIN.LÍL	Mullissu
dNIN.LÍL	Ninlil
dNIN.MAḪ	Ninmah
NIN-AN	Belet-šame
dNÍNDA.GU$_4$	Nindagud
dNIN-É.GAL	Belet-ekallim
dNIN-GARZA	Belet-parṣi
dNISABA	Nisaba
dNUMUN-DÙ	Ṣarpanitu
dNUN.GAL	Igigi
dPAPNUN	Tašmetu
dŠÀ.ZU	Šazu
dŠÁKKAN	Sumuqan
dŠEŠ.KI	Nannaru
dSIMUG	Ninagal
dŠÚ	Marduk
dTIŠPAK	Tišpak
dU.GUR	Nergal
dÙRI.GAL	Nergal
dÙRU-INIM	Uṣur-amassa
dUTU	Šamaš
dZUEN	Sin

APPENDIX G: CHRONOLOGY OF ASSYRIAN RULERS

The precise chronology of Assyrian kings—especially for the Old Akkadian and Old Assyrian periods—is often uncertain. The dates presented here are in line with those used in RIAo, though you should be aware that other probable reconstructions exist.

Old Akkadian and Ur III Eras

King	Reign	Extant Inscriptions
Ititi	?–? (23rd/22nd century)	1
Azuzu	?–? (23rd/22nd century)	1
Zarriqum	2050–2042	1
Son of Urdanum	?–? (21st century)	1
Aminu	?–? (21st century)	2
Ṣulilu	?–? (21st century)	1?
Kikkiya	?–? (21st century)	0
Akiya	?–? (21st century)	0

Old Assyrian Era

King	Reign	Extant Inscriptions
Puzur-Aššur I	ca. 2025–?	0
Šalim-aḫum	?–? (21st/20th century)	1
Ilu-šuma	?–? (20th century)	3

King	Reign	Extant Inscriptions
Erišum I	1974–1935	18
Ikunum	1934–1921	5
Sargon I	1920–1881	2
Puzur-Aššur II	1880–1873	0
Naram-Sîn	1872–1829/19	1
Erišum II	1828/18–1809	0
Samsi-Addu I	1808–1776	36
Išme-Dagan I	1776–1737	0
Sons of Nobody	1736–1730	0
Belu-bani	?–? (18th century)	0
Libaya	?–? (18th century)	0
Šarma-Adad I	?–? (18th–17th century)	0
Iptar-Sîn	?–? (18th–17th century)	0
Bazayu	?–? (17th century)	0
Lullaya	?–? (17th century)	0
Šu-Ninua	?–? (17th century)	0
Šarma-Adad II	?–? (17th century)	0
Erišum III	?–? (16th century)	0
Šamši-Adad II	?–? (16th century)	0
Išme-Dagan II	?–? (16th century)	0
Šamši-Adad III	?–? (16th century)	5
Aššur-narari I	?–? (16th–15th century)	10
Puzur-Aššur III	?–? (15th century)	9
Enlil-naṣir I	?–? (15th century)	2
Nur-ili	?–? (15th century)	0
Aššur-šaddûni	?–? (15th century)	0
Aššur-rabi I	?–? (15th century)	1
Aššur-nadin-aḫḫe I	?–? (15th century)	0
Enlil-naṣir II	1420–1415	0
Aššur-narari II	1414–1408	0
Aššur-bel-nišešu	1407–1399	2
Aššur-rêm-nišešu	1398–1391	7
Aššur-nadin-aḫḫe II	1390–1381	2
Eriba-Adad I	1380–1354	2

Middle Assyrian Era

King	Reign	Extant Inscriptions
Aššur-uballiṭ I	1353–1318	9
Enlil-narari	1317–1308	2
Arik-din-ili	1307–1296	8
Adad-narari I	1295–1264	51
Shalmaneser I	1263–1234	48
Tukulti-Ninurta I	1233–1197	57
Aššur-nadin-apli	1196–1193	3
Aššur-narari III	1192–1187	0
Enlil-kudurri-uṣur	1186–1182	0
Ninurta-apil-Ekur	1181–1169	2
Aššur-dan I	1168–1133	4
Ninurtal-tukulti-Aššur	1133	0
Mutakkil-Nusku	1133	0
Aššur-reša-iši I	1132–1115	22
Tiglath-pileser I	1114–1076	57
Ašared-apil-Ekur	1075–1074	0
Aššur-bel-kala	1073–1056	16
Eriba-Adad II	1055–1054	3
Šamši-Adad IV	1053–1050	5
Ashurnasirpal I	1049–1031	2
Shalmaneser II	1030–1019	1
Aššur-narari IV	1018–1013	0
Aššur-rabi II	1012–972	0
Aššur-reša-iši II	971–967	2
Tiglath-pileser II	966–935	2

Neo-Assyrian Era

King	Reign	Extant Inscriptions
Aššur-dan II	934–912	7
Adad-nerari II	911–891	11
Tukulti-ninurta II	890–884	21
Assur-nasirpal II	883–859	152
Shalmaneser III	858–824	131

King	Reign	Extant Inscriptions
Shamshi-Adad V	823–811	11
Adad-nerari III	810–783	42
Shalmaneser IV	782–773	4
Ashur-dan III	772–755	1
Ashur-nerari V	754–745	1
Tiglath-pileser III	744–727	77
Shalmaneser V	726–722	15
Sargon II	722–705	151
Sennacherib	704–681	261
Esarhaddon	680–669	183
Ashurbanipal	668–631	318
Ashur-etel-ilani	630–626	6
Sin-shar-ishkun	626–612	22
Ashur-uballiṭ II	611–609	0

APPENDIX H: OTHER VIEWS OF THE DATA

	Total	% Total	Occurrences	% Occur
Words	4,023	—	214,022	—
Nouns (n)	2,546	63.29%	110,594	51.67%
Verbs (v)	593	14.74%	36,445	17.03%
Adjectives (aj)	519	12.90%	13,172	6.15%
Adverbs (av)	240	5.97%	2,975	1.39%
Prepositions (prp)	35	0.87%	25,467	11.90%
Independent Pronouns (ip)	32	0.80%	2,172	1.01%
Numbers (nu)	15	0.37%	1,964	0.92%
Indefinite Pronouns (xp)	10	0.25%	328	0.15%
Modals (mod)	6	0.15%	3,810	1.78%
Interrogative Pronouns (qp)	6	0.15%	46	0.02%
Interjections (j)	5	0.12%	27	0.01%
Conjunctions (cnj)	4	0.10%	5,547	2.59%
Determinatives (det)	3	0.07%	5,725	2.67%
Demonstrative Pronouns (dp)	3	0.07%	269	0.13%
Subordinate Pronouns (sbj)	2	0.05%	248	0.12%
Reciprocal Pronoun (rp)	2	0.05%	101	0.05%
Relative Pronoun (rel)	1	0.02%	5,131	2.40%
Unknown (x)	1	0.02%	1	0.00%
Low-Occurrence Words				
4	194	4.82%	776	0.36%
3	256	6.36%	768	0.36%
2	401	9.97%	802	0.37%
1 (hapax legomena)	879	21.85%	879	0.41%
<5 Total	1730	42.99%	3225	1.51%

REFERENCES

Frahm, Eckart, ed. 2017. *A Companion to Assyria*. Hoboken, NJ: Wiley-Blackwell.

Hess, Christian W. 2020. "Standard Babylonian." Pages 471–88 in *A Companion to Ancient Near Eastern Languages*. Edited by Rebecca Hasselbach-Andee. Hoboken, NJ: Wiley-Blackwell.

Huehnergard, John. 2011. *A Grammar of Akkadian*. 3rd ed. Harvard Semitic Studies 45. Winona Lake, IN: Eisenbrauns.

Miller, Douglas B., and R. Mark Shipp. 2014. *An Akkadian Handbook*. 2nd ed. Winona Lake, IN: Eisenbrauns.